MASTER'S PLAN OF PRAYER

Learning to Pray As Jesus Prayed

Leslie B. Flynn

kregel
PUBLICATIONS

Grand Rapids, MI 49501

The Master's Plan of Prayer by Leslie B. Flynn

Copyright © 1995 by Leslie B. Flynn

Published by Kregel Publications, a division of Kregel, Inc.,
P. O. Box 2607, Grand Rapids, MI 49501. Kregel Publications
provides trusted, biblical publications for Christian growth
and service. Your comments and suggestions are valued.

Scripture quotations, unless otherwise noted, are from *The
Holy Bible: The New International Version* copyright © 1978
by the International Bible Society. Used by permission of
Zondervan Publishing House.

Cover photo: Adam Jones
Cover and Book Design: Alan G. Hartman

Library of Congress Cataloging-in-Publication Data
The Master's plan of prayer / by Leslie B. Flynn.
    p. cm.
  Includes bibliographical references.
  1. Jesus Christ—Prayers. 2. Prayer—Christianity. I. Title.
BV229.F57   1995   248.3'2—dc20   95-7845
                                                 CIP
ISBN 0-8254-2641-3 (pbk.)

      1 2 3 4 5 Printing / Year 99 98 97 96 95

Printed in the United States of America

Contents

Preface

The concert of prayer movement is currently gaining momentum across our country, as well as internationally. Increasingly, churches of various backgrounds join together for an evening of fervent intercession. Cutting through denominational and doctrinal differences, these concerts of prayer unite God's people in the common practice of seeking God's face for spiritual awakening and world evangelization. With this growing interest in prayer, it may be helpful to note how Jesus handled prayer in His personal life. In our naturalistic culture many see prayer as unrelated and unnecessary to the processes of buying, selling, working, shopping, getting an education, or investing in the stock market. Others echo the philosopher Santayana, "Prayer is painting your wishes against the clouds. When they happen true, you call it answered prayer. When they don't, you call it submission to the Almighty." But for multitudes of believers the simple fact that Jesus prayed is sufficient argument for the reality of prayer. If the strong Son of God, Creator and Sustainer of the universe, found it necessary to saturate His earthly ministry with prayer, how much more do His finite, faltering creatures need to pray! This is a not a book about prayer in general. Rather, this volume deals with prayer in the life of Jesus, and is limited to one aspect. Jesus taught about prayer, and He also practiced praying. The Gospels report both His sayings on prayer and also numerous occasions when He engaged in the exercise of praying. Many wonderful books have been written about Jesus and prayer, but most of these classics deal with both His teachings and His performances of praying. This book will not discuss His instructions for prayer, but will zero in on His actual deeds of praying. By this omission we do not imply that His teachings are unimportant or less important, but we suggest that the examples of His personal prayer life provide more than enough material for us to study and emulate. Sometimes a teaching is so interwoven with an act of praying that it must be included in the chapter discussion. For example, the Lord's prayer came as a result of the disciples' request after they overheard Him praying (see chapter 7). Following is a chronological list of the twenty-three recorded instances when Jesus prayed. Since prayer involves human emotion, and since Luke is the Gospel writer that emphasizes the human side of Jesus, it's not surprising that fifteen of the twenty-three instances are found in Luke; in fact, eleven occur only in Luke. These acts of His personal praying will occupy our attention in the later chapters.

- Luke 3:21 "When all the people were being baptized, Jesus was baptized too. And as he was praying, heaven was opened and the Holy Spirit descended on him in bodily form like a dove."
- Mark 1:35 "Very early in the morning, while it was still dark, Jesus got up, left the house and went off to a solitary place, where he prayed.
- Luke 5:16 "But Jesus often withdrew to lonely places and prayed."
- Luke 6:12 "One of those days Jesus went out to a mountainside to pray, and spent the night praying to God."
- Luke 9:16 "Taking the five loaves and the two fish and looking up to heaven, he gave thanks and broke them" (also Matt. 14:19; Mark 6:41; John 6:11).
- Mark 6:46 "After leaving them, he went up on a mountainside to pray" (also Matt. 14:23).
- Mark 8:6–7 "When he had taken the seven loaves and given thanks. . . . They had a few small fish as well; he gave thanks for them also. . . ." (also Matt. 15:36. Only Mark mentions the double thanks).
- Luke 9:18 "Once when Jesus was praying in private and his disciples were with him, he asked them, 'Who do the crowds say I am?'"

- Luke 9:28–29 ". . . He took Peter, John and James with him and went up onto a mountain to pray. As he was praying, the appearance of his face changed, and His clothes became as bright as a flash of lightning."
- Luke 10:21 ". . . Jesus, full of joy through the Holy Spirit, said, 'I praise you, Father, Lord of heaven and earth, because you have hidden these things from the wise and learned, and revealed them to little children'" (also Matt. 11:25).
- Luke 11:1 "One day Jesus was praying in a certain place. When he finished, one of his disciples said to him, 'Lord, teach us to pray.'"
- John 11:41–42 "Then Jesus looked up and said, 'Father, I thank you that you have heard me. I knew that you always hear me. . . .'"
- Matthew 19:13 "Then little children were brought to Jesus for him to place his hands on them and pray for them" (also Mark 10:16).
- John 12:27–28 "Now my heart is troubled, and what shall I say? 'Father, save me from this hour'? No, it was for this very reason I came to this hour. Father, glorify your name!'"
- Luke 22:17, 19 "After taking the cup, he gave thanks . . . And he took bread, gave thanks and broke it. . . ." (also Matt. 26:26–27; Mark 14:22–23).
- Luke 22:31–32 "Simon, Simon, Satan has asked to sift you as wheat. But I have prayed for you, Simon, that your faith may not fail."
- John 17:1 "After Jesus said this, he looked toward heaven and prayed" (Then follows Jesus' intercessory prayer uttered on the way to Gethsemane—the entire chapter).
- Luke 22:39–46 "Father, if you are willing, take this cup from me; yet not my will, but yours be done" (v. 42). Jesus prayed this petition three times in Gethsemane (also Matt. 26:36–44; Mark 14:32–42).
- Luke 23:34 "Father, forgive them, for they do not know what they are doing" (first cry from the cross).
- Matthew 27:46 "My God, my God, why have you forsaken me?" (fourth cry from the cross; also Mark 15:34).
- Luke 23:46 "Father, into your hands I commit my spirit" (seventh and final cry from the cross).
- Luke 24:30 "When he was at the table with them, he took bread, gave thanks, broke it and began to give it to them."

- Luke 24:50–51 "When he had led them out to the vicinity of Bethany, he lifted up his hands and blessed them. While he was blessing them, he left them and was taken up into heaven."

Jesus was a man of prayer. In addition to His regular times of prayer, every major episode of His ministry found Him lifting His voice to heaven: at His baptism, at the selection of the Twelve, at His Transfiguration, at the feeding of the five thousand and four thousand, at the raising of Lazarus, in Gethsemane, on the Cross, and at His Ascension. Prayer dominated His life. The accomplishments of His ministry came through His praying. Through prayer He was able to complete His Father's will. As important as the fact of Jesus' praying is the manner of His praying. How did Jesus pray? When? Where? Why? For what? The purpose of this book is to analyze the principles of Jesus' prayer life in order to adopt them into our own devotional practices. Patterning our prayer life after His model will help us pray Jesus' way.

Here are some questions to be discussed:

- Were Jesus' prayers prepared or extemporaneous?
- Why did Jesus seem not to pray for the salvation of people, nor tell us to pray for the salvation of others?
- How did Jesus address God in virtually every one of His direct-quote prayers?
- Did He ever get "no" for an answer?
- Were His prayers long or short?
- Did He ever pray for an hour or longer?
- Did He always pray on His knees?
- Did He ever reveal any request made in His private praying?
- How frequently did He offer prayers of thanks?
- Did His prayers mainly have subjective value (His shining face in the Transfiguration), or objective value (getting results and accomplishing things)?
- When Jesus told us to pray in a closet with door shut, did He literally mean that we should pray in an enclosed space?
- What were some of the places where Jesus prayed?
- Jesus prayed for His disciples as a group, "Those whom You gave Me." But did He pray for His disciples by name?

- Did Jesus have a regular hour to pray? If so, what time of day?
- Did He ever pray in times of trouble?
- Did Jesus depend on prayer alone?

The answers to these questions should help start us on the way to pray as Jesus prayed. For example, saints have always been impressed with the episode of Jesus rising very early in the morning and going out to pray. Consequently, morning prayer has been a habit of countless Christians in all ages. Many pursue the same practice in our generation. Author Charles Swindoll says, "Many a morning I begin my day by sitting on the side of the bed and saying: 'This is Your day, Lord. I have no idea what these next twenty-four hours will contain. But before I begin, before I sip my first cup of coffee, even before I get dressed, I want You to know that from this moment on, I'm Yours. Help me to be a branch that abides in the vine, that draws strength from You. Take control of my senses so that I am filled with Your presence and power.'"[1]

Jesus' unanswered prayer in Gethsemane to be spared the cup has brought comfort to countless saints whose earnest prayers have hit against the brick wall of a silent heaven. A good friend of mine, Dr. Arthur H. Lewis, who resigned his teaching post at Bethel College after a disabling stroke four years ago, now publishes *Biblical Reflections*, studies for pastors, teachers, and Bible students.

In his 1994 winter issue he deals with unanswered prayers. He begins with a testimony of answered prayers in his life, reviewing his combat experience as a bombardier on thirty-four missions over Germany in World War II, including the day he had to parachute from his burning B-17 before it crashed. He mentions how God heard his prayers for a clear memory and wisdom when he faced "those impossible exams at Harvard and Brandeis (Hebrew, Syriac, Akkadian, and Ugaritic) in pursuit of his doctorate in Semitic languages. He cites other answers: the right partner to share his life and work, the many blessings through fifteen years of missionary service in Portugal, the birth of three children, five grandchildren, and for protection and safety on so many overseas trips.

Then he tells of the stroke that crippled his left leg and took the strength from his strong left hand. Repeatedly he prayed for

God to free his body of its weakness, but no answer came. So he made a study of unanswered prayer in the Bible, including Jesus' earnest, repeated petition in the garden to avoid the suffering He knew was coming the next day.

As a result Lewis sees that "God's 'No' always has a reason and that His will in the end works for our good." He confidently states, "Now my faith is challenged to wait for the return of Christ for the full answer to my prayers."[2]

Jesus often prayed in the presence of His disciples. He intended they should learn and profit from His prayer habits. No one ever spoke as Jesus as Jesus spoke. Neither did anyone ever pray as Jesus prayed.

Dr. A. S. Simpson, founder of the Christian and Missionary Alliance, said, "The mystery of prayer! There is nothing like it in the natural universe . . . Marvelous bond of prayer which can span the gulf between the Creator and the creature, the infinite God and the humblest and most illiterate child."[3]

No one did it better than Jesus. By praying Jesus' way we can enrich our prayer life privately and also publicly in Concerts of Prayer. We begin by addressing this question: Why did Jesus pray when He was being baptized?

Notes
1. Charles Swindoll, "Fuel for the Journey" in *Moody Monthly*, February 1994, p. 27.
2. H. Lewis Lewis, *Biblical Reflections*.
3. A. S. Simpson, *When the Comforter Came* (Camp Hill, Pa.: Christian Publications, 1911).

CHAPTER 1

Praying at the Start

At the 1988 Congressional Breakfast in Washington D.C., Billy Graham told a story about a company president who said to his secretary one morning, "Let no one in to see me until I tell you it's all right." Moments later along came the chairman of the board who was told that the president had an important appointment and couldn't be disturbed. Despite the secretary's protestations, the board chairman angrily pushed through the doors of the president's office, and saw him on his knees. Tiptoeing out, in a subdued voice he asked the secretary, "Does this happen often?" She replied, "This is the way he begins each day." The president's practice of putting prayer at the top of his office agenda doubtlessly enabled him to face with composure and confidence the frenzy and frustrations that awaited him that day. From a study of Jesus' prayer life we learn that it's a wise practice to pray at the start of a new episode, challenge, crisis, or phase of life.

At His Baptism Which Signaled the Start of His Earthly Ministry

Only Luke records the fact that Jesus prayed at his baptism. "When all the people were being baptized, Jesus was baptized too. And as he was praying, heaven was opened" (3:21). From the emphasis Jesus later put on prayer it's safe to assume that this is not the first time He prayed. Praying to His Father was probably as natural as breathing, but this is the first mention of Him praying.

Jesus prayed because He was about to begin his public ministry. Immediately following his baptism we read, "Now Jesus himself was about thirty years old when he began his ministry" (Luke 3:23). The original simply says, "when he began", but the NIV adds the obvious, "his ministry." The four Gospels deal essentially with His three-year public mission. Though His birth and related incidents are given, the first thirty years are silent, except for brief mention of his visit to the temple at age twelve, when He confounded the doctors. In his introduction to Acts, Luke speaks of his Gospel as "my former book" in which "I wrote about all that Jesus began to do and to teach until the day he was taken up to heaven" (1:1–2). The real story begins at age thirty, signaled by His baptism, and ending with His ascension.

A person was judged to reach maturity at thirty. Joseph was thirty when he stood before Pharaoh to begin his great work as prime minister of Egypt (Gen. 41:46). At age thirty Levites entered into their priestly ministry (Num. 4:3, 23), and according to some commentators scribes could lawfully begin to teach. Since John the Baptist was six months older than Jesus (Luke 1:36), he probably had been ministering to the crowds at least half a year before he baptized Jesus. So it's not surprising that at age thirty Jesus began his ministry as High Priest and Prophet. Baptism marked the introduction of this new, important phase of His life. How natural for Him to pray on such an important occasion, which has been described variously as the dedication, consecration, ordination, anointing, installation, investiture, or the divine inauguration of Jesus to the mission of bringing eternal life.

When Joseph and Mary returned from the flight into Egypt, they settled in Nazareth (Matt. 2:22). Mark's first historical reference to Jesus says He "came from Nazareth in Galilee and was baptized by John in the Jordan" (1:9), implying that Jesus had lived in Nazareth from infancy. How long was Jesus to be known as a carpenter in the town of Nazareth? The time had come for Him to embark on His public ministry which would lead to the cross. So He made His debut.

How baptism portrayed His coming ministry

His baptism was part of fulfilling all righteousness. Nature performs many of her finest tasks slowly and silently, like the growing of grass, the coloring of leaves, and the blossoming of flowers. During the years as Jesus grew in stature, in knowledge, and in favor with God and man, especially from His twelfth year on when He had told His parents that He must be about His Father's business, He was increasingly aware that the day would come when He would have to bid farewell to Nazareth and go on to a larger ministry. He needed some sign.

Then He heard of John the Baptist, the ascetic who suddenly emerged from the solitary life of the wilderness sternly preaching repentance and warning his hearers to flee from the wrath to come. It was a time of great excitement and eager expectation. As the multitudes thronged the Baptist, Jesus felt an inner compunction to join this Godward movement, and present Himself for baptism. He knew that the hour had come.

Though John did not yet recognize Jesus as the Messiah, he did understand that his cousin was a singular man. Likely aware of the unusual events surrounding His birth, probably told to him by his own parents, Elizabeth and Zacharias, and familiar with Jesus' character, John, who had declared himself unworthy of untying Jesus' shoes, urgently tried to hinder Jesus from His request, replying in effect, "I, who administer the baptism of repentance, need to profess repentance myself, and should rather receive baptism at your hands, who are so much holier than I." John wanted to change places.

Jesus replied that at this moment it was His duty to be baptized by John, and John's duty to baptize Him. He did not deny His superiority, but asked John to let Him have the inferior position. Each, by submitting to his own respective responsibility, would do the righteous will of God. Jesus kept His record of keeping godly customs solid. Circumcised the eighth day, presented in dedication in the temple, He now yielded to the rite of baptism, eager to keep all the Father's commands.

By His baptism, He identified with sinners. Certainly Jesus was not baptized to symbolize the forgiveness of His sins, for he had no sins to forgive. Why, then, was He baptized? He was baptized to show His identification with sinners. Jesus joined the sinners coming to John the Baptist to signal the nature of His earthly ministry. He had come to bring relief to sin-burdened humanity. So He mingled with sinners, befriended sinners, died between sinners. If He was to be numbered with transgressors, why not join them at the outset of His ministry? His baptism was a representative act which foreshadowed the Cross where He would be made sin for us (2 Cor. 5:21) and by which He would purge our sins.

His baptism signified a new direction in life. Baptism is a picture of death and resurrection—death to the old life and resurrection to a new order. Baptism looks backward and forward. Jesus was now leaving His home in Nazareth and embarking on a new career.

Baptism is often called an initiatory rite, symbolizing one's entrance into the Christian faith. It is generally accepted that for Jesus baptism constituted His formal acceptance of His Messianic duties, an act which would require the complete leaving of His peaceful, private life and the giving of Himself to a new, public, itinerant ministry. Baptism marked the official opening of His ministry. Giovanni Papini in *Life of Christ* said, "He did not go down to the Jordan to cleanse Himself, but to show that His second life was beginning."[1] One commentator heads this section of Scripture, "The Hour Strikes for Jesus."

His Praying

Why did He pray? A momentous task confronted Him. For thirty years He had lived a life of obscurity and calm. Now He was to be thrust into a tumultuous assignment, traveling from place to place with nowhere to lay His head, thronged by fickle crowds, finding it difficult to eat and rest from His labors of teaching and healing, fiercely dogged by opponents whose hatred would lead to gruesome crucifixion. His prayer likely contained two elements: a statement of consecration to the ministry before Him, and a request for divine strength to carry it out.

Jesus dedicated Himself to His Father's will. Perhaps it would be more accurate to say that He rededicated Himself. Just before He left heaven to be born in Bethlehem, He said, "I have come to do your will, O God" (Heb. 10:7). At age twelve, when rebuked by His parents for getting lost on a Passover trip, He replied that

He had been about His Father's business (Luke 2:49 KJV). Now was the time for Him to act on His Father's commission, and He was ready, even to sacrifice His own life.

Standing on the brink of new responsibility, He may have prayed something like this, "I have come to do Your will, O Father. The teachings, the miracles, the healings, the dialogues, the confrontations, the associations with the least, lowest, and lost, the sufferings and death, the entire ministry I now dedicate to You. See Me through. May I finish My course, on which I now embark, with obedience, joy and triumph."

Alfred Edersheim in *The Life and Times of Jesus the Messiah* suggests that Jesus may have adopted the opening parts of the Lord's Prayer such as, "My Father which art in heaven . . . Thy kingdom come. Thy will be done in earth, as it is in heaven." Edersheim says that this prayer had been a part of Jesus' inner life long before He ever taught it to His disciples.[2]

Jesus requested divine strength. Jesus is to enter strange scenes, engage in new services, and encounter severe struggles. Stupendous issues hinge on His actions. Right after the baptism He will be led into the wilderness to be tempted by the devil. He will need strength. If Edersheim is correct in his conjecture about Jesus using phrases from the Lord's prayer, a later petition would have been most apropos, "Deliver Me from the evil one. For Thine is the kingdom and the power."

On the threshold of assuming His role as Prophet, Priest, and King, Jesus prayed for the graces, gifts, power, and authority which the stress and storms of His great calling would demand.

The Answer to His Praying

"And as he was praying, heaven was opened and the Holy Spirit descended on him in bodily form like a dove. And a voice came from heaven: 'You are my Son, whom I love; with you I am well pleased'" (Luke 3:21–22). The grammar suggests that Jesus continued praying as He was emerging from the waters until interrupted by the opening of the heavens. The descent of the Holy Spirit in the form of a dove and the voice of His Father from heaven were the answers to Jesus' two petitions.

The Spirit's Descent. The Holy Spirit in the bodily form of a dove hovered over Jesus, then landed and remained on Him (John 1:32–33). The dove, a harmless, sensitive bird that would not settle on anything unclean, typifies innocence, gentleness, and purity. Jesus had prayed for help. Now He had all the resources of the Supreme Helper. Previously Jesus doubtless knew the presence of the Spirit, but now all the graces and gifts of the Spirit would reside in Him without limit (3:34), enabling Him for all that was to follow.

Immediately the Spirit became active in His life. The Savior returned from the Jordan full of the Holy Spirit (Luke 4:1). He was then led by the Spirit into the desert for His victory over the Tempter (4:1). Then He returned to Galilee in the power of the Spirit (4:14). Entering the Nazareth synagogue, He read the Scripture, "The Spirit of the Lord is on me" (4:18). Later when the Seventy returned with reports of victory over Satan, Jesus offered a prayer, full of joy through the Spirit (10:21).

Because Jesus had the abiding authority of the Spirit, never would He be powerless to heal the sick, nor thwarted by demons, nor bamboozled by the arguments of opponents, nor too tired for the task, nor bewildered by the crowds, nor unnerved by enemy plots. Never would He be diverted from the path before Him. The dove was the emblem of the power by which He would speak as no other had ever spoken, display compassion as none other, and then die as no one else had ever died, the just for the unjust. The night before He died, He was able to say to His Father, "I have brought you glory on earth by completing the work you gave me to do" (John 17:4). Because of His prayer at the start, He was able at the end to rejoice in a mission accomplished.

We note the involvement of all members of the Trinity: the Son submitting, the Spirit descending, and the Father approving.

The Father's Voice. A voice from heaven, heard by Jesus and John, and perhaps clearly only by them, said, "You are my Son, whom I love; with you I am well pleased" (Luke 3:22). This is a combination of two quotes, one from Ps. 2:7 which speaks of crowning the son of David as Messiah, the other from Isa. 42:1 which refers to the ideal Servant of God who perfectly does His will while walking the pathway of obedience and service, culminating in the sufferings of Isaiah 53.

This commendation has been called the Father's "ordination formula." The Father is saying, "I certify You as My Son. I place my stamp of approval, not only on the thirty years to date in which no deflection from the path of obedience has occurred, but I accept Your dedication for the three-year public ministry ahead." It was the Father's solemn validation of the person and dignity of the Son and of the career He was about to enter. In short, the Father was pleased with the obedience of His Son who had just dedicated Himself to fulfilling the Father's program.

Three times the Gospels record the Father's voice speaking from heaven: here at the baptism, at the transfiguration (Luke 9:35), and at the visit of the Greeks (John 12:28). In every case the voice came after a prayer by Jesus. And all three cases involved the cross. Jesus' baptism was a picture of death and pointed to Calvary. At the transfiguration the conversation centered on Jesus' death. To the Greeks Jesus spoke of seed falling into the ground and dying, and of His lifting up, a reference to the way He would die. In every instance the Father's voice would bring encouragement and strength to His Son and propel Him toward the ultimate event for which He had come to earth—the offering of Himself as a sacrifice for sin on the cross.

As a result of His praying, Jesus emerged from the Jordan heavenly-gifted and heavenly-affirmed. The rending of the sky would point to the closeness of His Father whose presence Jesus repeatedly sought in lonely moments (John 16:32).

Jesus' prayer shows that "the time of all times to pray is on life's threshold. Not after we have tried and failed, and God looms before the soul as a possible last resort, but in life's magic dawn, when all Nature wears a halo, and Hope is boundless, and the soul is charged with the romance and glory of life's first beginnings—that is the time of times to pray!"[3]

Jesus, who received the Spirit's strength in answer to His baptismal prayer, has promised the same Holy Spirit to those who ask (Luke 11:13). Prayer for the Spirit's fresh filling at the commencement seasons of life is a wise procedure. Here are occasions where prayer may launch us into fruitful service.

At the Start of the Christian Life

On a visit to Asia, Dr. Donald Grey Barnhouse met a lady whose husband owned a million-dollar business. Though both were believers, their son was a notorious playboy. Dining in their home, Barnhouse invited the young man to the service that night. At the meeting the young man professed faith in Christ. That night he prayed earnestly for strength to live a new life.

The next day he had the following notice printed in English and Chinese, then mailed to his friends and business contacts, "Hob Ong, having given his life yesterday to Jesus Christ as Lord and Savior, sends this announcement to his friends and acquaintances, that he will no longer be seen in the haunts he has been accustomed to frequenting." His prayerful decision at the beginning of his new life helps explain the years of faithful discipleship that followed.

At the Start of New Building Projects

Nehemiah spent time in prayer before rebuilding the walls of Jerusalem. Four months elapsed between the stirrings of his secret desire to help his people and his open request to the king (Neh. 1:1–2:8). It may seem lopsided to spend four months praying about a project which would take less than two months to complete (6:15). But Nehemiah was a man of prayer before he was a man of action. Prayer helped him withstand later opposition.

How fitting for a church, erecting a new sanctuary or educational unit, to begin each stage with a prayer of consecration, whether ground-breaking, cornerstone-laying, or completion of the structure. Pastor and people should ask the Lord to make that building a place where the Lord is worshiped, the Word is taught, saints are edified, sinners are converted, and from which missionaries are sent forth.

How well I recall a couple who asked me to come one Saturday to dedicate their newly purchased, renovated home. How fitting it is to offer a prayer of consecration at this new landmark and to join in singing the musical number, "Bless This House."

At the Start of Various Ministries

Before the church at Antioch sent out Barnabas and Paul on their first missionary trip, the congregation fasted, prayed, laid hands on them, and sent them away (Acts 13:3). Before Paul started his second missionary tour, he and Silas, were "commended by the brothers to the grace of God" (15:40). Likely all such junkets were preceded by petition for divine enduement. One missionary educator confessed, "I used to think that prayer should have the first place and teaching the second. I now feel it would be truer to give prayer the first, second, and third places, and teaching the fourth."

How impressive it is at ordination services to see several pastors surround the kneeling candidate, place hands on his head, as someone beseeches the Lord to give him "an exemplary character, an enlightened mind, and a burning heart."

A highlight of my denomination's annual convention is the commissioning of missionaries. At this service, up to thirty, mostly young people, educationally qualified and graduates of rigorous examination, are publicly acknowledged by the official boards as missionary appointees for foreign, home, or chaplaincy service.

Fitting occasions for corporate church prayer include the launching of an evangelistic crusade, a Bible or missionary conference, a visitation, or stewardship campaign.

At the Start of Life's Milestones

Newlyweds need prayer as they *begin their married* life for the resolve to keep their vows, the long-suffering to get along, the skill to communicate, and the ability to overcome all problems as partners in the covenant of companionship.

The thought of *raising children* should send a couple to their knees. Thinking over fifty-five years of married life, Bob and Jean Walker, each an only child, and Jean virtually disowned on announcing her conversion, recall their early prayer, "Lord, we have no brothers or sisters. We pray for a family of children to love and who will love us in the days ahead." The Lord gave them five children, and a host of grandchildren.

Before the birth of a baby, how vital it is to pray for its safe and healthy arrival, and for a divinely-guided career. On the Sunday evening I accepted Christ as my Savior, at the age of fifteen, my mother said to me as we walked home from church, "Son, I prayed for this night before you were born."

With all of life before a baby, how fitting it is to offer a prayer of *infant dedication*, something like this, "Lord, You who took little ones in Your arms, bless this child. May she be strong in body, alert in mind, stable in emotions, and early come to know the Savior who invited little ones to come to Him." Jesus took children in His arms, and prayed for them (Mark 10:16).

How often my wife and I, about to *begin a trip*, crowded in our station wagon with seven little daughters and suitcases, have bowed our heads to ask for safety. "Please keep Daddy alert, and protect us from careless drivers and accidents."

Ezra, about to lead a group of emigrants on a very dangerous journey from Babylon to Jerusalem, refused an armed escort, despite their cargo of 28 tons of silver. Since he had told King Artaxerxes that God would protect His own, a military guard would demonstrate a lack of faith. So, before leaving he prayed for safety from bandits. They arrived in Jerusalem with every life spared and all the treasure intact (Ezra 8:21–32).

As a boy, I heard a student, home for summer from a college, testify how the night before *school opening* the previous fall he had gotten on his knees to ask the Lord to see him through the year, and how the Lord had been faithful. A few years later, the night before the start of every year of college and seminary, I asked the Lord to help me pass my courses, and He did.

Teachers in Christian schools often open their *classes* with prayer. One of my professors always offered this petition before every exam, "Grant calmness of heart, retentiveness of memory, and facility of expression."

Taking a seat in a *church service*, one man invariably prays, "O Lord, I am in Your holy house. Help me to focus my thoughts so that I may worship You with full devotion." One lady, as she opens her Bible for *private worship*, regularly asks, "May the Holy Spirit shed divine light upon the sacred page."

Vaughn Shoemaker, for many years cartoonist for the *Chicago Daily News*, and twice Pulitzer prize winner, went to his knees every morning before starting work. He would not dream of creating a cartoon without first thanking God for his God-given talent and asking God to guide his hand as he began to draw.

Other milestone events, suitably preceded by prayer, include *starting a new job, moving to a new location, celebrating a birthday or wedding anniversary,* or *undergoing surgery.* One pastor, on his seventy-fifth birthday, prayed, "Lord, I ask Your blessing on this first day of the last quarter century of my life."

Our Daily Bread tells of a well-known surgeon in a large hospital who always spent a few moments alone before entering the operating room. One day an intern, getting up courage, asked the specialist if there might be a relationship between his surgical success and pre-surgery solitude. The surgeon replied that there was a definite connection. "Before each operation," he explained, "I ask the Great Physician to guide my hands. On many occasions I am confronted with very delicate situations or unexpected conditions in my patient, and I hardly know what to do next. At such times I immediately become conscious of God's help. He always gives me the wisdom I need to complete the surgery successfully. I never take my scalpel in hand without first seeking His aid."[4]

At the Start of a New Year

The *threshold of a new year* can be an emotional time. No one knows what the new year has in store: health or illness, prosperity or adversity, peace or war, success or failure, life or death? Only God knows. The future is in His hands.

Many people celebrate the arrival of a new year in a God-forgetting way, following the adage, "Eat, drink, and be merry, for tomorrow we die." But devout Christians have a wiser approach. Meeting with others in worship during final hours of the year, they mark the passage of time by pondering the brevity of life and making resolutions. Many of God's people leave these services, revived in spirit to face an uncertain future, and to buy up the opportunities for doing good.

A story in *The Pentecostal Evangel* tells of a group of drinkers gathered in a noisy hotel barroom where liquor was flowing freely. One of those present was the local pastor's wayward son, imbibing moderately. During a pause in the revelry Joe, the town's hardened skeptic, walked in.

"They're having a Watch Night service over in the church," he said, stamping the snow from his boots, and taking a drink. "I don't see why we can't have one here." Then, mocking a ministerial tone, he continued, "Brother Eldrige, will you please lead in prayer?" Eldrige, a glib-tongued barber, caught up the joke, dropped to one knee, and with folded hands gave a mock prayer. "And now we'll sing a hymn," continued Joe, sounding so like the local preacher that it brought a roar of laughter from the crowd. He led a church hymn, as others joined in raucously.

With the hymn finished, Joe continued, "Brother Sam will now preach the sermon, and we trust it'll be for the spiritual good of us all." To Sam, the local preacher's wayward son, this was a most disagreeable assignment. Making a rush for the door, he was intercepted, and given an ultimatum, "Preach now or treat every man here." Sam had no money, so had to try giving a sermon.

When he stalled by saying he had no text, someone shouted, "Try 'the spirit is willing, but the flesh is weak.'" Sam began by mumbling that in spite of good intentions they would find that the flesh was indeed weak, that they had better make a break with the old sinful ways and start a new life. It came out so strongly that Joe said, "Why, I believe the fool's in earnest."

Sam had not been sincere at first, but now seemed genuine. He began to say things suppressed by years of godless living. Fragments of his deceased mother's prayers, Bible verses from Sunday school, truths he had heard his father say—all now came tumbling out from his lips with new force. The others at first were resentful, then surprised, then interested. Even the most intoxicated suddenly sobered, and all listened in silence.

Before Sam knew it, he was down on his knees on the barroom floor, asking the Lord to forgive him. Two other men were genuinely converted that night, leaving sober and serious. Joe, though making no public confession, was never again heard to mock the Christian faith.

As Sam turned a corner on his way home from the barroom, he overtook his aged father, feebly making his way home from his Watch Night service. What joy for both when Sam took his father's arm and told him his prayers had been answered. His father spent the rest of the night on his knees, thanking God.[5]

Senate Chaplain Richard C. Halverson says that the following quotation from Minnie Louise Haskins has held a profound personal significance for him, as each new year begins,

"I said to the man who stood at the gate of the year: 'Give me a light that I may tread safely into the unknown.'

"And he replied: 'Go out into the darkness and put your hand into the hand of God. That shall be to you better than light and safer than a known way.'"

Missionary George Kelsey says that usually in their Watch Night service in Amman, Jordan, he shares "a verse for the year that indicates partially the direction of our preaching and target of ministry for a new year. Last year we meditated on John 13:34 and tried to encourage a spirit of love."

At the Start of the Day

Jesus asked the blessing *before meals*. He prayed all night *before selecting His apostles*. He looked heavenward *before doing His miracles*. He invoked God's help *at the start of the day*.

The day may be the smallest division of God-given time. Seconds, minutes, and hours are manmade and artificial, but the astronomical day, the period required for the earth to make one complete revolution on its axis, is a product of nature—seemingly the shortest span of time God has provided.

The emphasis on the day in Scripture highlights it as a very important division of God-given time. The Lord daily bears our burdens (Ps. 68:19). He gave the Israelites manna sufficient for a day. We are to pray for our daily bread. The Bereans searched the Scriptures daily (Acts 17:11). We are to exhort one another daily (Heb. 3:13), and to take up our cross daily (Luke 9:23). The psalmist cried unto the Lord continually (86:3).

If the day is such a significant interval, how important to start it with prayer. We are not surprised to read, "Very early in the morning, while it was still dark, Jesus got up, left the house and went off to a solitary place, where he prayed" (Mark 1:35). Facing the opportunities and battles of the day, Jesus chose the early morning for prayer. At that time the mind is fresh, often at its clearest, free from distraction, and able to concentrate. Early prayer sanctifies the entire day, helps overcome its temptations, and provides strength for its duties.

Before going to bed, the captain in the private dining room of a venerable New York City club has said the same "Now I lay me down to sleep" prayer that he learned as a child in the Bahamas. Seldom getting to bed before 1 a.m., he needs this prayer to give assurance of God's keeping through the night. "But even more important," he says, "is the prayer that I say in the morning. So it is that years ago—38 of them, I think—a prayer formed in my mind. And I've said it every single morning since.

> Now I'm awake and see the light.
> God has kept me through the night.
> Unto Him I lift my voice and pray
> That He might keep me through the day.

—Edmund L. Johnson[6]

Even before rising we may place ourselves in the Lord's hands. One man said, "I pray before I get out of bed in the morning. As soon as I awake, I roll over on my stomach, place my head in my hands, and praise the Lord for what He has done and is going to do."

Charles Whiston, in his book *Pray: A Study in Distinctive Christian Praying*, offered this morning prayer, "O Lord Jesus Christ: in obedience to Thy holy claim upon me, I give myself anew to Thee this day; all that I am, all that I have; to be wholly and unconditionally Thine for Thy using. Take me away from myself, and use me up as Thou wilt, when thou wilt, where You wilt, with whom Thou wilt. Amen."[7]

A more formal prayer reads, "O God, give me strength to live another day. Let me not turn coward before its difficulties or prove recreant to its duties. Keep me sweet and sound of heart, in spite of ingratitude, treachery, or meanness. Preserve me from minding little stings or giving them. Help me to keep my heart clean, and to live so honestly and fearlessly that no outward failure can dishearten me or take away the joy of conscious integrity. Grant me this day some new vision of truth, inspire me with the spirit of joy and gladness, and make me the cup of strength to suffering souls, in the name of Jesus."[8]

Predawn prayer meetings have been a characteristic of the church in Korea from its inception. A survey of three hundred evangelical pastors discovered that 100% of the one hundred responding said they engage in daybreak prayer, with about 80% spending up to an hour in personal prayer following the church session. About 10% of the congregation attend regularly, which means that an attendance of 250 to 300 is not unusual. All over the nation thousands of believers gather every morning beginning between 4:40 and 5:00 a.m. Pastors attribute much of the growth of Korean Christianity to early morning prayer someone started fifty years ago. A little boy puzzled his parents by insisting that he would not get out of bed until he could see Jesus. When he pointed to a painting of Jesus on the wall, it dawned on them—he wouldn't get up till it was light enough to see the face of Jesus.

A personal letter from a seminary official ended, "May His gracious presence be the place where you start each day."

His Ascension—The Start of His Heavenly Ministry

Just before Jesus ascended, He prayed over His disciples. In fact, He was still blessing them when He was taken up into heaven (Luke 24:50–51). It would be natural to conclude that He was praying a farewell benediction at the end of His earthly ministry, and to comment that Jesus prayed both at the start (baptism) and finish (Ascension) of His earthly mission. But the Ascension did more than conclude His work on earth; it also initiated His heavenly ministry. Jesus was praying for a new task involving a continuation of His earthly association with His apostles. He had worked with His disciples on earth; He was still going to work with them but from His heavenly position.

Luke opens the book of Acts where his Gospel leaves off. He begins, "In my former book, Theophilus, I wrote about all that Jesus began to do and to teach, until the day He was taken up to heaven. . . ." (1:1–2). In his Gospel he wrote about what Jesus did and said while *on earth*. The implication is that in his new book (Acts), he is going to write about what Jesus is still doing since arriving *in heaven*. Luke's Gospel recounts His earthly ministry; Acts deals with His heavenly ministry. The Ascension, mentioned in both Luke 24 and Acts 1, divides the two missions.

Before Jesus began His heavenly ministry, He prayed. For what did He pray? Likely His blessing on the disciples included some of the same elements of His High Priestly Prayer: their protection, unity, fruitfulness, and the coming of the Spirit for empowerment. He was about to inaugurate the dispensation of the Holy Spirit, who, though eternally existent and operative in Old Testament times, was now to come in a special way. Jesus had promised to send the Holy Spirit (John 14:16) to convict, regenerate, seal, lead, sanctify, teach, indwell, and empower. Just before He ascended, He told His disciples to wait at Jerusalem for the Spirit whose power would enable them to be His witnesses to the ends of the earth. The promise of the Spirit was fulfilled at Pentecost when 3,000 believed in the Messiah. The rest of Acts is an account of the triumphant travels of the apostles who went everywhere proclaiming the good news. Jesus' final earthly prayer was amply answered. The fifth book of the New Testament should be called *The Acts of the Risen Christ by the Power of the Holy Spirit through His Apostles.*

The final verses of Mark (16:19–20) put it this way, "After the Lord Jesus had spoken to them, he was taken up into heaven and he sat at the right hand of God. Then the disciples went out and preached everywhere, and the Lord worked with them and confirmed his word by signs that accompanied it."

Before the curtain went up on His new, heavenly ministry, Jesus' blessing encompassed all His future works, not only those by His apostles, but also those which continued down through the centuries by all His servants, till He comes again.

Notes

1. Giovanni Papini, *Life of Christ* (New York: Harcourt, Brace & Co., 1923), p. 61.
2. Alfred Edersheim, *The Life and Times of Jesus the Messiah*, vol. 1 (Grand Rapids: Wm. B. Eerdmans, 1943), p. 283
3. John Henry Strong, *Jesus, The Man of Prayer* (Valley Forge, Pa.:Judson, 1945), pp. 25–26.
4. *Our Daily Bread*, Radio Bible Class, Grand Rapids, April 28, 1988.
5. *The Pentecostal Evangel*, December 1956.
6. Edmund L. Johnson, *Guideposts*, May 1991, p. 27.
7. Charles Whiston, *Pray: A Study in Distinctive Christian Praying* (Grand Rapids: Wm. B. Eerdmans, 1972).
8. *Prayers New and Old*, (Cincinnati: Forward Movement Publications, n.d.), p. 24.

CHAPTER 2

Finding Quiet

A young couple, recognizing the need for a quiet time for individual prayer, tried an experiment. In the evening, one watched the youngsters while the other went into the bedroom to pray. After a half hour they exchanged places. The plan never worked. The wife would hear the squeak of a linen closet door opening in the hallway outside. Knowing that her toddler could empty the lower shelves, she kept hoping for someone to close it. Then the phone rang and kept on ringing. She thought, "Someone answer, please." Before she knew it, the half hour was up.

One day a neighbor told about his new job at the airport. "The noise of those jets is unbelievable. I wear ear protectors like a headset." His wife thought, "Headset?" A few evenings later, alone in the bedroom, she adjusted a pair of stereo headphones. The change was remarkable. She couldn't hear a thing. "Lord, I thank You," she prayed. "Now I can tune You in."

Jesus Prayed at a Quiet Time in a Quiet Place

After a busy day in Capernaum

Though Jesus didn't have jet noise hammering His ears, He did know the pressure of busy days and mammoth crowds from the start of His tours. After an action-packed Sabbath in Capernaum,

"Very early in the morning, while it was still dark, Jesus got up, left the house and went off to a solitary place" (Mark 1:35).

Jesus began that busy Sabbath by teaching in the synagogue. His hearers were amazed because, unlike the usual teachers of the law, He taught with authority. In the midst of His discourse He healed a demoniac who shook violently as the shrieking demon was cast out. The crowd was so astonished that when the service was over they spread the news all around the surrounding area.

Leaving the synagogue, Jesus went to Peter's home where Peter's mother-in-law was sick in bed. The diagnosis, according to Dr. Luke, was a high fever (4:38). Jesus healed here. The cure was instantaneous. She began to wait on them.

As word of both healings spread like wildfire to the homes of the ill and demon-possessed, relatives gathered up their sick and brought them in the cool of the sunset, after the Sabbath was over, and placed them at the door of Peter's house. It seemed everyone in town was there, hundreds and hundreds. *The Pulpit Commentary* says, "What a motley multitude must have been there! The consumptives were there, with pale face or hectic flush; victims of incurable cancer were there; persons with the burning heat and the parched lips, or in the very delirium of fever were there; the palsied, the dropsical, the epileptics were there; patients having diseases of the heart, of the lungs, of the head, of the spine were there; the lame, the dumb, the blind, were there. Some were able to walk, some on crutches, some were mounted on asses, and some carried on pallets by friends or neighbors. Demoniacs, too, were there. . . ."[1] Jesus went through the suffering throng and healed them all. It had been a day packed with activity, typical of many to come.

After His sleep, Jesus felt the need to pray. His busy day had drained His emotional and spiritual reserves. He wanted a quiet time, away from everybody. So He rose while it was still dark, estimated at between 3 and 6 a.m. He went off to a solitary place. Solitary can be translated lonely, deserted, waste, uninhabited, abandoned, desolate. The verbs "got up" and "went off" indicate more than a mere wishful attitude but decisive action on the part of Jesus to find a secluded spot at a tranquil hour. Both time and place show that Jesus went to great length to avoid distraction in order to pray. It wasn't enough to find a quiet spot in the house.

You help bring Jesus to thousands of lives each day through the outreaches of CBN. Thank you ... and may God bless you.

Dear Diane,

Scripture tells us, "The fruit of the righteous is a tree of life, and he who wins souls is wise" (Proverbs 11:30, NIV).

Thank you for helping CBN reach lost souls in America and around the world. Your gifts have enabled us to touch millions with the love of Christ. Do you have a need we can pray about? If so, please call CBN's prayer line at (800) 759-0700.

Please send in a gift today to help reach those who are waiting to hear the Good News!

977 Centerville Turnpike
Virginia Beach, Virginia 23463
24-hour Prayer Line (800) 759-0700
www.CBN.com

The purpose of this card is simply to provide you with an easy way to give and record your gifts to CBN. If you've already mailed your gift this month and do not wish to make a special gift, just disregard this card. You'll receive another gift card next month to use if you desire. In the meantime ...

- If your address is incorrect, please note it on the front and provide your correct address in the space provided above.

- If you're moving soon, send us your new address ahead of time so we won't miss you in the transition.

- If you're getting duplicate mailings, return both cards to us and indicate which address information is correct.

Thank you for helping us keep our records accurate and for your continued support of this ministry. May God bless you.

He must have had in mind a session of some length, for no one rises so early and goes so far for a just a few moments of casual prayer.

Why did He pray at this hour and in this place? First, Jesus needed to recharge His spiritual batteries. Although the day before He had displayed power over disease and demons and had taught with such evident authority that an entire area marveled, He knew that great tasks awaited Him, even that day, and for His Galilean campaign, for which He must seek renewed strength. Exhausted spiritually by the previous day's activities, prayer was indispensable. Prayer would fit for more work; then completion of work would require more prayer.

Retirement to solitary places was as truly a feature of Jesus' ministry as periods of breathless activity. Some scholars find ten definite withdrawals from public service which indicate ten separated periods of His teaching tours. But His private praying wasn't confined to the ten times He began new preaching crusades. It's likely He found a quiet time to pray each day.

If the holiest and grandest Person who ever graced this globe needed communion with His heavenly Father, how much more do we? Our need of prayer for our own teaching and ministry requires the habit of a definite time and the appropriate "closet."

The second reason Jesus prayed in that solitary place was for direction in His work. His popularity endangered His ministry. Captivated by His healing power, people were missing the real import of His teaching. He knew the tendency of many to elevate physical health above spiritual health. But He also knew that losing one's soul was infinitely worse than living this life in an ill body. Perhaps He prayed that the real message would not be lost in all the excitement of miracles. Did He ask, "Is all this fame because of healing really compatible with My mission?"

Some years ago a leading Korean evangelist, whom the missionaries were convinced had the gift of healing, announced to their surprise that he was giving up his healing ministry. He explained, "God has called me to evangelize, but people are now beginning to come to me, not to be evangelized, but only to be healed." Perhaps Jesus experienced some of this apprehension.

After healing a leper

The next incident in Jesus' ministry was the healing of a man covered with a severe case of leprosy, a loathsome and terrible disease with progressive ulceration, which gives the victim a grotesque appearance. A leper was banished from towns and villages, required to wear a covering over his mouth, and to warn of his approach by crying, "Unclean! Unclean!" Jesus healed this leper and commanded him not to tell anyone except the priest. Instead, the leper went out and talked freely. More people came to be healed of their sicknesses. Again, the growing crowds hindered Jesus' preaching. And again, Jesus sought out a desolate area. Luke says this retreat to quiet was a regular habit, ". . . Jesus often withdrew to lonely places and prayed" (5:16). He needed to renew His strength to prevent any depletion of His spiritual power and to pray for guidance.

One writer pictures Him saying, "Father, My human ego is really gratified by all the fame I'm receiving, but I'm on this earth to do Your will. Father, what should I do? Should I stay and bask in the popularity, or should I move on and deliver Your message to Israel?"[2] These prayer times do not seem to follow a prearranged schedule, but whenever He felt a need to pray He would escape to private spot. It's also likely that He broke away toward the close of each day, especially when we learn later that it was His habit to pray evenings in Gethsemane when in the Jerusalem area. In fact, assuming that He had a regular morning and evening prayer quiet time would not stretch credulity.

Several others times we are told that Jesus sought quiet. Some references we will simply list, since they receive treatment in later chapters.

Choosing the Twelve

Jesus sought privacy in the hills to pray all night before choosing the Twelve. "One of those days Jesus went out to a mountainside to pray, and spent the night praying to God" (Luke 6:12). See chapter 3 of this book.

After feeding the 5000

After the miracle of the loaves and fishes which fed the 5000, the crowd wanted to make Him king. Because of this developing crisis Jesus ordered the Twelve to take a boat across Galilee ahead of Him, dismissed the crowd, and then, "After leaving them, he went on a mountainside to pray" (Mark 6:46). (See also Matt. 14:23 and chapter 5).

Before Peter's confession

Once near Caesarea Philippi "when Jesus was praying in private and his disciples were with him, he asked them, 'Who do the crowds say I am?'" (Luke 9:18). This was just prior to Peter's magnificent confession of Jesus' deity (see chapter 5). Many times Jesus prayed by Himself, but often He took His disciples along with Him and prayed within their hearing.

At the transfiguration

"He took Peter, John and James with him and went up onto a mountain to pray. As he was praying, the appearance of his face changed, and his clothes became as bright as a flash of lightning" (Luke 9:29). See chapter 6.

When the disciples asked Him to teach them to pray

"One day Jesus was praying in a certain place. When he had finished, one of his disciples said to him, 'Lord, teach us to pray, . . .'" (Luke 11:1). See chapter 7.

His intercessory prayer

Jesus offered what is known as His High Priestly Prayer on the way to Gethsemane (John 17). See chapter 8.

In Gethsemane

The specific locations of the Galilean hills where Jesus went to find quiet have not been given us, but we do know of a favorite spot in the Jerusalem area. From the Upper Room on the night of His betrayal "Jesus went out as usual to the Mount of Olives, and His disciples followed Him" (Luke 22:39). He led them about 50 yards beyond the brook Kidron to a garden, called Gethsemane, situated at the lower slope of the Mount of Olives. It was His custom to come here evenings. That's how Judas knew where to find Him to betray him to the Sanhedrin. Amid the fresh breezes and coolness of the thick foliage, Jesus would find refuge as He turned to the Father in prayer. On this last night before His death He preferred the solitude of the garden to the confusion of Jerusalem. Preserved to this day, with eight venerable olive trees dating back several centuries, the garden still maintains a historical feel.

Previously when His travels had taken Him to the Jerusalem area, He had frequently prayed outdoors in the Olivet area before sleeping outdoors. Sometimes friends invited Him to stay overnight. Often He had no place to lay His head.

For example, John 7 tells of Jesus' earlier visit to the Feast of Tabernacles and relates what happened at the end of the day as everyone headed home. Visualize Jesus and a few disciples, making their way through the Jerusalem streets at dusk after a busy day of temple teaching. As doors open to receive His followers into their homes for the night, the group slowly thins out till only two or three remain. Finally, one remaining disciple turns into his house. Only Jesus is left. Though evening meals are about to be served, no friendly call beckons Him in. The last verse reads, "Then each went to his own home." The first verse of the next chapter completes the record, "But Jesus went to the Mount of Olives" (John 7:53; 8:1). The Savior walks on alone, passes through the city gate and over the brook Kidron to find a resting place beneath the gnarled, knotted olive trees on the slope of Olivet. Perhaps some kind voice had invited Him in, but He turned it down, sensing the need to pray.

During the final week Jesus taught daily in the temple, retreating evenings to Gethsemane to spend the night. He would pray before retiring, and again early in the morning before resuming the rigors of another day. Some scholars suggest that Mary, mother of Mark, owned the property and gave Jesus right of entry. For more on Jesus praying in Gethsemane, see chapter 9.

Our Need for Quiet

The roar of aircraft, the rush of traffic, the frantic pace of the marketplace, and the din of thumping stereos all seem to be raising the decibel level of our already noisy world. If Jesus sought respite from the hectic harassment of relentless mobs, we need to carve out a piece of quiet for prayer.

A Quiet Time

Quiet may come from time as well as place. Early prayer not only gives strength for the battles that follow, but also provides privacy for contemplation. Something spiritually therapeutic flows from morning quiet before the world gains possession of our thoughts. Without it the day often goes wrong.

Old Testament characters rose early to pray.

- Abraham rose early to stand before the Lord (Gen. 19:27).
- Job rose early to intercede for his children (Job 1:5).
- Jacob rose early to worship the Lord (Gen. 28:18).
- Moses rose early to meet God (Ex. 34:4).
- Gideon rose early to talk to God (Judges 6:38).
- David directed prayer upward in the morning (Ps. 5:3).

Christian leaders of earlier generations rose early to pray.

- Martin Luther said, "If I fail to spend two hours in prayer each morning, the Devil gets the victory through the day."
- John Wesley rose at 4 a.m. to spend two hours in prayer and meditation each morning. He traveled on horseback 4,500 miles annually, as many as 8000 in a single year. He gave more than 40,000 sermons a year. He said, "I have so much to do that I must spend several hours in prayer before I am able to do it."

One traveler said that the most moving experience of his "life was stepping from John Wesley's bedroom in his London house into the little prayer room adjacent. Outside the house was the traffic noise of City Road, but in that prayer chamber was the holy hush of God. Frankly, I am not one who is easily moved by atmosphere, but in that little room I was moved. The only furnishings are a walnut table with a Greek Testament and a candlestick, a tiny prayer stool, and a chair. It was here that Wesley would come early each morning (when he was in London), read God's Word, and pray. 'This little room was the powerhouse of Methodism,' the guide whispered."

- John Calvin began his work at 6 a.m., preceded by prayer.
- Charles Simeon rose each day to pray from 4 to 8 a.m.
- Timothy Dwight, who entered Yale at thirteen and taught there at nineteen, used to rise at 4 a.m. for prayer and study.
- E. M. Bounds, who wrote the classic *Power Through Prayer* rose at 4 and prayed till 7 a.m. He wrote from a full heart.
- Bishop Asbury said, "I propose to rise at 4 a.m. as often as I can and spend two hours in prayer and meditation."
- As a youth, William Booth, founder of the Salvation Army, wrote several resolutions on a scrap of paper. The first one read, "I promise God that I will rise early every morning to have a few minutes—not less than five—in private prayer."

Before the discovery of electricity and modern heating people went to bed earlier, and thus rose earlier. But today we have our lights, central heating, and evening engagements, so most of us do not rise as early as saints of an earlier century.

We have *examples from this century*.

- Dr. J. Oswald Smith, missionary statesman and founder of Peoples Church in Canada, said in late life, "For over sixty years now I have observed the morning watch. Because I meet God in the morning, I solve my problems before I come to them. Without the morning watch my work would be weak and helpless."
- When president of Wheaton College, Dr. V. R. Edman said, "I find it imperative to begin my day early in order to accomplish the day's task. Perhaps my wife and I are extremists in that

regard. We find it very helpful to arise by four o'clock in the morning, perhaps a little earlier. We have a cup of coffee and a sweet roll or doughnut at that hour, and then take at least an hour and a half for uninterrupted devotional reading of the Scripture and prayer together. The phone never rings at that time of the morning and there are no other interruptions."

- Dr. George Palmer, founder of the Morning Cheer broadcast and Sandy Cove Bible Conference, used to rise early enough to pray one hour for his daily radio program, known for its theme chorus, "Jesus Never Fails."
- John Ashcroft, Governor of Missouri, starts his day early in prayer with his wife and children. At 7:45 a.m. in his office he joins a small group of government workers for Bible study and prayer. On Sunday he attends an Assembly of God church.

A Quiet Place

Because Jesus knew the value of seclusion, He urged His disciples, "When you pray, go into your room, close the door and pray" (Matt. 6:6). Must we literally go into a closet to pray? Though it might be the answer for many, it could be a another locale. What is important is to have a place, a private place, and usually the same place, easily reachable. One man put a note on his front door, "Don't go to the trouble of knocking. I am at home but I will not open the door." Another hung a sign on his office door, "In Conference with the Boss."

For many in first-century Galilee the fig tree was their closet. Growing 15 feet high, the tree spread its branches outward to 25 feet. Since many houses had only one room, those who wanted privacy sought the shade of the fig tree. Meeting Nathaniel for the first time, Jesus told him that He had seen him under his fig tree, meaning, in meditation (John 1:47–48).

On his travels in China, Hudson Taylor, founder of the China Inland Mission, would sleep in the poorest of inns. At night he would screen off, as his quarters, a corner of the large room, filled with other travelers. In the morning, long before others awoke, he would light his candle, read his Bible, and pray.

For A. W. Tozer a dingy corner of the basement of the family home became his private prayer chamber.

Don Landaas, a member of the elite Marine Ceremonial Guard on helicopter sentry duty at Camp David the weekend President Eisenhower was entertaining England's Prime Minister Macmillan, disobeyed regulations. Wanting solitude, he slid back the door of Eisenhower's helicopter, sat down, and began to pray. Discovered inside, he was sent back to Washington for disciplinary action. On trial he could have claimed that he was investigating a noise in the helicopter, but he said, "Colonel, I went in there because I wanted to pray. As a Christian I have dedicated myself to my Master just as you, a colonel in the Marine Corps, are a man dedicated to your commander." Because of the serious nature of his act, he was given a sentence, though suspended. Two weeks later, Landaas, an accomplished accordion player, auditioned with the Marine Band, and was appointed accordion soloist for the rest of his military hitch. Three months later, when Eisenhower returned to Camp David for weekend talks with Krushchev, Landaas was one of six musicians chosen to go along, ironically flying up in the same helicopter group he previously guarded, including the one in which he had prayed.

One pastor finds praying on a two-mile early morning walk on a lovely avenue most rewarding, though concentration is often broken by traffic and other walkers. One walker wears earphones (turned off) so people will not engage him in conversation. One man makes the cemetery his place of devotion in good weather. Another gets in his car, drives, parks, and prays. Still another just keeps driving. One Sunday he testified in an adult Sunday School class, "I do some of my best praying while I'm driving." Immediately the voice of his wife was heard to remark, "I, too, do my best praying while you're driving."

At sunrise an alarm clock rings in a Pennsylvania farmer's bedroom. Donning overalls, he goes to the barn and prays.

In a midwestern hospital a Christian surgeon hangs up his coat jacket, then slips into a side room to spend a few moments alone in prayer before entering the operating room.

A mother on the west coast locks herself in her bedroom for twenty minutes each morning to intercede for her family. A father descends to the living room before the family awakes.

A business man goes early to his office. Another heads for a rarely used elevator in his apartment, stops it between floors, and pours out his soul. An unused walk-in closet was converted into a prayer room. A cleaned-up coal cellar was likewise transformed. With space at a premium in many homes, a favorite chair or table has become a familiar place of prayer. When business slacked at her outdoor vegetable stand on a main highway, the lady proprietor would flip her expansive apron over her head and pray silently amid all the clamor of traffic.

Richard J. Foster in *Prayer: Finding The Heart's True Home* says that he often uses the first part of a plane flight for worship, prayer, and meditation. One winter he scheduled a three o'clock appointment into his date book for each working day, drove to the local zoo, and spent fifty minutes on a bench in a lovely indoor rain forest in meditation.[3]

Some denominations have retreat centers where individuals or groups come for a day or weekend of spiritual refreshment.

Prayer leaders recommend that churches open early in the morning for prayer. A designated room could contain lists of requests.

Solitude Pays Dividends

As a man thinks in the quiet of his heart and in the solitude of his closet, so is he. How important to have a private devotional communion to stir up love for Jesus and neighbor.

Solitude helps us concentrate. One enemy of prayer is mind-wandering. Our truant imagination flips from topic to topic. Boisterous children, ringing phones, blaring commercials, rigid deadlines, and a dozen voices vie for our attention. The quiet place is an oasis in the midst of our distractions. Someone said, "Unless a man takes himself out of the world by retirement and self-reflection, he will be in danger of losing himself in the world." External silence cultivates internal serenity, preparing the heart for prayer.

Solitude helps us sense danger. Two animal lovers, walking along the banks of a river, could hear the subdued rush of falling water. One remarked that birds, seemed scarce. The other, a professor of zoology, replied, "Animal life is always sparse near a waterfall.

The small creatures, birds, and fur bearers don't like to stay near a place where the roar of a cataract may mask the sound of danger." In today's rush we need to find the quieter haunts, lest the enemy's approach goes unnoticed. Like Jesus, who left the crowds to find a private place, we should seek the secret place of the Most High and abide under the shadow of the Almighty.

Solitude eliminates showing off. For some in Jesus' day prayer had been reduced to a pious show. Jesus called the Pharisees hypocrites, literally, actors. They performed their prayer-act in public, using street corners, marketplaces, or temple as a stage to show off their holiness. Some made long prayers while cheating widows out of their homes (Mark 12:40).

To counteract the sham, Jesus warned, "But when you pray, do not be like the hypocrites, for they love to pray standing in the synagogues and on the street corners to be seen by man. . . . When you pray, go into your room, close the door and pray to your Father, who is unseen. Then your Father, who sees what is done in secret, will reward you" (Matt. 6:5–6).

Jesus was not forbidding public praying. He Himself prayed before thousands. He is scrutinizing not method but motive. The insincerity of praying in order to fake piety drew His harsh rebuke. The verb "to be seen" gives us our English "theater." Jesus' insistence on privacy cuts through theatrical grandstanding. How could anyone enter a private room to pray with pretense? With no one around, whom would he be aiming to impress? Certainly not God who sees through fakery. Seclusion encourages an honest, intimate relationship.

Solitude forces us to face ourselves. Some people want it always noisy so they awaken to the radio, wear headphones, drive with the car stereo blaring, work with background music, keep the TV going all evening, and go to sleep with music playing in their ears. Constant noise keeps them from thinking about their problems. But at times we need to stop and face reality.

Commentators suggest that the desert is a powerful biblical image of an inhospitable place without lambs, but with scorpions and thorns—by day the intense heat and sun glare—by night the bitter cold. The desert was the place to which Jesus often withdrew. There, after His baptism, He spent forty days of fasting (and doubtless, praying), amid the wild animals, successfully withstanding the lures of the Devil (Mark 1:12–13).

The desert is a place that helps us look deep within our own heart, discover our shortcomings, and turn to the Lord for help. It's not a place of escape from reality, but of entrance into deeper reality—a place of terror but yet of victory. Solitude can be a place where you find yourself and God.

Solitude helps us refuel. A major reason Jesus withdrew was to revitalize His reserves, depleted by the exhausting demands of busy days, teaching His disciples privately and crowds publicly, interacting with inquirers, performing miracles, walking great distances, comforting the brokenhearted, and reaching out to sinners. Retirement to pray reveals His source of power.

Busyness, even in a ceaseless round of church activity, can cause frazzled nerves, irritable dispositions, and deadly fatigue. Prayer was something Jesus seemed to do before and after service. A proverb says, "A holy life does not live in the closet, but it cannot live without the closet." Christlike praying in secret is the secret of Christlike living in public. To fail to spend time in prayer is as foolish as a pilot saying before a flight, "I've so much to do that I don't have time to put fuel in the plane."

Albert Barnes, author of *Notes on the Old and New Testaments*, declared "that the religious enjoyment through the day will be according to the state of the heart in the morning, and can therefore be measured by our faithfulness in early secret prayer"[4] Incidentally, Barnes wrote all of his commentaries before 9 a.m., bathing them in early prayer.

The secret place is where we gain our victories. Luther, asked about his plans for the morrow, said, "Work, work, and more work from early until late. In fact, I have so much to do that I shall spend the first three hours in prayer." The prophet said, "In quietness and trust is your strength" (Isa. 30:15).

Maintaining a Quiet Time and Place Requires Discipline

An ad showed a man sitting down to an enticing bowl of cereal, saying, "I get up 15 minutes earlier to do this." Some get up earlier to jog, or catch an earlier bus to work. Many have made the decision to rise earlier to spend time in prayer. But it will take action as well as resolve. A young preacher who found it difficult to get up asked an older pastor, "Do you pray about getting up?" "No," came the answer, "I just get up."

A student at Cambridge University signed a pledge for early morning devotions, so he rigged a contraption over his bed. When his alarm went off, a sponge dripped cold water on his face.

A new Christian asked prayer-warrior George Muller to pray for him to get out of bed earlier, so he could pray in the early morning hours. Muller replied, "You get one leg out, and I'll ask the Lord to get the other one out!"

In his book, *A Serious Call to a Devout and Holy Life*, the Puritan William Law advised, "If you were to rise early every morning, as an instance of self-denial, as a means of redeeming your time, and fitting your spirit for prayer, you would find mighty advantages from it. It would keep it constantly in your head, that softness and idleness were to be avoided, that self-denial was a part of Christianity. It would teach you to exercise power over yourself, . . . and make you able by degrees to renounce other pleasures and tempers that war against the soul."

Many link prayer to bedtime when they recited, "Now I lay me down to sleep." A cartoon shows a little girl telling her pal that she prayed that morning for a fun day. Her pal comments, "You prayed this morning? Most people pray at night." The first girl explains, "The lines are less cluttered in the morning."

Not everyone is a morning person, but those who choose bedtime for their quiet time should beware, lest tired and sleepy, they mumble through a brief petition or two before hitting the hay, giving the Lord the leftovers of time.

Isaac chose to meditate in the evening, retreating to a field to get away from family and herdsmen (Gen. 24:63). He found it refreshing to pray in the hush of twilight as the stars began to appear. He had lots to pray about as he lamented his mother, anticipated a bride for whom Eleazar had gone searching, and concerned over possible confrontation with the Philistines over well ownership.

A biographer of C. S. Lewis says that Lewis liked to be home by five p.m. for a pot of tea, then go to his bedroom and wash up. "If there was not already one in his room, he would then ask for a Bible 'in any translation' and say his prayers. He found this the best time of day for them. If he left them till later, he was usually too sleepy."⁵ Though Lewis prayed in the morning too, he apparently preferred the evening hour.

Many pray both morning and night. Daniel "three times a day . . . got down on his knees and prayed" (Dan. 6:10). As a devout Jew, Jesus likely prayed morning, afternoon, and at sunset. Some prayer books contain prayers for morning, noon, and night. Any hour is the proper time when solitude is available. Despite her many duties, Susanna Wesley, mother of Charles and John, found time to pray from one to two every afternoon. More important than when or where is the fact itself. In modern life busy schedules will often dictate choice of time for quiet time.

Though never far from the public eye and the tumult of the crowd, Jesus found quiet. Often He stayed up late. Sometimes He rose early. He disciplined Himself, and expects us to do the same. He said, "When you pray," not "if you pray." He desires us to enter the closet and say, "Lord, I have shut the door."

Richard Baxter in his *Saints Everlasting Rest* counseled us to find the fittest time for prayer—that time of day when we are most alert, the fittest place for prayer—that place in which we can be all alone with God, and the fittest preparation of heart.

Failure to make rendezvous with the quiet place can ultimately prove disastrous. A fable tells of a soaring bird which, spotting a piece of sweet food, asked how he could get it. Told to surrender a feather, he plucked one out and received the sugary morsel. What mattered one feather? But after trading feather after feather for tasty tidbits, he noticed that he could not soar as easily. And then, one day, he discovered he could no longer fly. To neglect the closet may keep us from rising to the heights the Lord intended.

But they that wait upon the Lord "will renew their strength. They will soar on wings like eagles; they will run and not grow weary, they will walk and not be faint" (Isa. 40:31).

Notes
1. *Mark*, vol. 1 of *The Pulpit Commentary*, new edition, (New York: Funk & Wagnalls Co.), p. 76.
2. Curtis C. Mitchell, *Praying Jesus' Way* (Grand Rapids: Revell, 1991), p. 19.

3. Richard J. Foster, *Finding the Heart's True Home* (San Francisco: HarperCollins, 1992), p. 74.
4. Albert Barnes, *Notes on the Old and New Testaments* (Grand Rapids: Baker, 1974), p. 332.
5. George Sayer, *Jack—C. S. Lewis and His Times* (New York: Harper & Row), p. 207–209.

CHAPTER 3

Increasing the Missionary Force

On a recruiting visit to a prominent evangelical seminary, a missionary executive discovered that during the first half of that school year one hundred students were seriously preparing for missionary service. Naturally, the missionary executive wondered how there could be such a high level of missionary interest on the campus. Then he learned the reason. Every day at noontime a missions professor met with a band of students to pray for missions and for expanding interest among other students in the Great Commission.

Jesus' Strategy—Prayer for Increase in the Labor Force

The professor was following Jesus' strategy for increasing the church's labor personnel. One day as Jesus looked at the crowds surrounding Him, He was moved with compassion because "they were harassed and helpless, like sheep without a shepherd. Then He said to His disciples, 'The harvest is plentiful but the workers are few. Ask the Lord of the harvest, therefore, to send out workers into His harvest field'" (Matt. 9:36–38). The verb translated "send out" has a strong meaning, literally "to cast out, eject by force, expel, thrust out, drive out, push out." Believers are to pray urgently for workers to be shoved out into the overflowing harvest fields of the world.

Jesus modeled His own strategy by praying for a new category of workers. Luke relates, "One of those days Jesus went out into the hills to pray, and spent the night praying to God. When morning came, He called his disciples to Him and chose twelve of them, whom He also designated apostles" (Luke 6:12–13). What was the reason for the all-night prayer session? Jesus was facing a momentous decision. He needed a special class of laborers, a group of men who would leave their homes to be His constant companions for three years, who would submit to His training, who would go forth to carry the gospel to other nations, and who as His apostles would form the foundation of the New Testament church. Whom from among His followers should He choose? So Jesus prayed, and He prayed all night.

The various concerns which caused His prayer

In political and business life the success of any venture depends not only on the talents of the administrator, but also on his ability to select subordinates to enthusiastically carry out his program. Jesus' dilemma was compounded by these concerns.

The enormity of the enterprise

Never were men to be chosen for so important an assignment. Jesus' mission was to reach to the uttermost parts of the world, and to influence the welfare and destiny of all the generations to come. The time to train His workers was limited. Although they would be intimately associated with Jesus for three years, after that they would be deprived of His visible presence and thrust into the task of proclaiming, explaining, and defending the gospel, establishing and edifying churches, and enduring persecution.

An old legend imagines Jesus arriving in heaven right after the Ascension, welcomed by all the angels. Then the angel Gabriel asks Jesus, "You suffered much, dying for the sins of mankind. Does everyone down there on earth know it?"

"Oh, no," replies the Savior, "just a handful of folks in Jerusalem and Galilee know about it."

"Well, Master," continues Gabriel, "what is Your plan for everyone to know of Your great love?" The Master replies, "I asked all My apostles to carry the message into all the world. I told them to tell others, who will in turn tell others until the last person in the farthest corner has heard the story." Gabriel's face clouds, for he spots a flaw in the plan. "What if after a while Peter forgets and goes back to his fishing on Galilee? What about James and John and Andrew? Suppose Matthew returns to his tax booth in Capernaum, and all the others lose their zeal and just don't tell others. What then?" After a pause comes the calm voice of Jesus: "Gabriel, I have no other plan."

Looking over the nondescript, ragtag, dullish, unlearned group of would-be followers, seemingly destined for oblivion, He might have wondered which ones possessed the potential of becoming members of a band of flaming and courageous evangelists who within three decades would spread the Good News through much of the Roman Empire, winning disciples even in Nero's palace. No wonder Jesus prayed, and prayed all night.

The deficiencies of these men

Jesus was fully aware of the imperfections of the group of men from whom He had to choose His apostles. He knew they were slow learners. He wasn't surprised when they later showed fear during a violent storm on Galilee. He saw their lack of faith. He realized their ambitions to occupy important offices. He sensed their streak of cowardice which could lead to denial of longtime friendship. He knew that Peter lacked stability. He wasn't caught off guard when James and John wanted to incinerate a town.

Peter Marshall in a sermon "Disciples in Clay" pictured the apostles appearing before an examining board appointed to choose Jesus' close associates. Peter stood there, uncouth and impulsive, smelling of fish. Andrew, James, and John also reeked of fish oil, and lacked refinement. Philip appeared indecisive. Judas was a thief. Simon the Zealot had belonged to the revolutionary freedom-fighters, and perhaps harbored some natural animosity against Matthew who had sold himself into the service of Rome as a tax collector, thus earning the reputation of traitor to his country. Without whitewash, the New Testament paints them as they were: a group not "most likely to succeed."

Had the Twelve done the choosing, they might have rejected each other. But Jesus was doing the choosing. Knowing that He would have to rely on throne-climbers and deserters, bumbling men with all their failures, faults, and foibles to accomplish His mission, no wonder He prayed.

The requirement of teachability

Doubtless Jesus had keen insight into the hearts of people, enabling Him to read character at a glance. He knew all about the shortcomings of His potential apostles, but He also knew that with the right kind of spirit and patient, prolonged teaching, they could be trained and transformed. Through uninterrupted companionship He would fashion them into a select band. The indispensable quality would be teachability.

Certain types were ruled out. He couldn't choose snobbish millionaires, imperious socialites or know-it-all academicians. Picture a dozen rich men dressed in expensive clothes, with gold-filled wallets, trying to communicate Jesus' warnings on the dangers of wealth, or His love for the poor. He could not select twelve scholars whose degrees would keep them from sitting at the feet of Jesus to learn simple but essential lessons.

A Salvation Army girl, witnessing in a crowded train, sweetly said to a dignified gentleman, "Sir, I hope you are a Christian." Slightly befuddled, he replied, "Why, I am a theological professor." The simple girl, earnestly placing her hand on his arm, said, "Sir, don't let that stand in your way."

Those whom Jesus chose would have to be poor in spirit, pliable, childlike, unpretentious, humble, men. Although slow to learn, they had to be willing to learn. If filled with their own knowledge, they would have no room for His wisdom. So He wanted teachable followers. Traveling with Him, they would catch His heart of tenderness, grasp His goals and sacrificial spirit. Although missing the erudite training of advanced schooling, three years under His tutelage would provide an unsurpassable education, making them anything but theological illiterates.

A high school senior, desperately wanting admission to a certain university, wrote on her application, "I'm not a leader, but I think I am a good follower." The admissions officer replied, "Applications for our freshman class indicate that there are 599 leaders coming to the college next fall to fill 600 openings. We feel that the college is required to admit one follower. Please be advised that your application is accepted." Jesus was looking for followers in order to make them leaders.

Jesus prayed all night. This is the only recorded instance of Jesus engaging in all-night prayer, though He may have done so at other times. "All night" is a medical term to describe the urgency of a doctor's all-night vigil at a patient's bedside. Jesus faced this crisis with a long prayer vigil.

All night is a long time to pray. Many American believers have not experienced an entire night of praying, including myself. The nearest I came to it stemmed from an emergency phone call a little after midnight from a Christian doctor two thousand miles away, informing me that my daughter had unintentionally overdosed, was hovering between life and death, and to pray. My wife and I prayed much of the night, and in the morning heard the good news that she had pulled through.

Would a minister be thought peculiar if he asked from the pulpit for concerned members to meet with him for prayer beginning at 10 p.m. Wednesday night till 4 a.m. for the selection of a teacher for their large college class, a ministry that would impact the lives of collegians for years to come?

The answer. As morning dawned, the crisis was over. Jesus knew whom to select. With wisdom given from above He chose from among His followers twelve men whom He designated apostles. Luke lists their names (6:14–16). When one became a traitor, another was chosen in his place. The Twelve fulfilled their assignment.

But more workers were needed beyond the twelve apostles. So Jesus later "appointed seventy-two (seventy, according to some manuscripts) others and sent them out two by two ahead of Him to every town and place where He was about to go." Still more harvesters were required. So again He gave the command, "The harvest is plentiful, but the workers are few. Ask the Lord of the harvest, therefore, to send out workers into His harvest field"

(Luke 10:1–2). Likely it was an oft-repeated injunction. The prayer for workers must still be made today.

May there be a definite tie-in between prayer and the supply of the Christian labor force? When missionary societies have a shortage of candidates, or when the local church cannot find teachers for the Sunday school, is it because we are substituting manmade recruitment methods for God's program of prayer? When God ordains the salvation of the lost, He also ordains the means. Prayer for workers is a major link in God's chain of instruments.

Note a distinction. Jesus didn't instruct His followers to pray for the harvest, but for harvesters to reap the harvest. Strangely, the teaching of Jesus lacks any substantial body of specific commands to pray for the salvation of the lost, even though His concern for the lost is well-documented. Sinners He sought. He wept over Jerusalem. He forgave the dying thief. He came to earth to die to save the lost. He was moved with compassion over shepherdless sheep. Lack of instruction to pray for lost people cannot be blamed on any deficiency in His concern. May not the key to Christian service, home or abroad, center less on asking for a harvest than on praying for harvesters who, burdened for the harvest, go forth to reap?

One veteran Christian leader observes, "After many years in the ministry associating freely with prayer groups from every level of Christian society, I think I can safely state that there are probably ten petitions uttered for the salvation of lost sinners (the harvest) for every one uttered for the thrusting forth of laborers into the harvest. Yet in the Scriptures, Christ explicitly and definitely taught the latter but never explicitly and definitely the former. Does this not indicate how far afield the emphasis of our current prayer practice is from the teachings of the New Testament?"[1] In keeping with Jesus' command, should not the accent be on talking to God about raising up laborers greatly concerned about the harvest? Doesn't New Testament strategy indicate that God normally uses human instruments (harvesters) to win the lost.

Jesus' strategy was continued in the early church

Almost every chapter in Acts mentions prayer. Several times prayer involved the choosing and sending of a harvester. When in the Upper Room it came time to choose a successor to Judas, and two names were proposed, "Then they prayed, 'Lord, you know everyone's heart. Show us which of these two you have chosen to take over this apostolic ministry'" (Acts 1:24–25). Matthias was chosen. From then on he was counted among the Twelve, and joined in many significant campaigns as a harvester.

When the number of disciples so increased at Jerusalem that more workers were needed to oversee the daily distribution of food, prayer was involved in the dedication of these new laborers (6:1–6), and doubtless in their choice.

At Caesarea the godly centurion Cornelius was praying when the Lord told him to send for a man named Simon, also called Peter, then staying at the home of Simon, the tanner, by the sea in Joppa. Peter, readied by a vision before the delegation's arrival, went with them to Caesarea where he became God's harvester in Cornelius' household (chap. 10).

When Peter was in prison scheduled for execution the next morning, the church met in the home of Mary, mother of John Mark, and prayed all night for his release. God knocked off Peter's chains and opened the iron gate for his release. The church had been praying, not for a new laborer to begin his ministry, but a veteran apostle to be able to continue his reaping (12:1–17).

When the growing church at Antioch was fasting, and likely praying, the Spirit said, "Set apart for me Barnabas and Saul for the work to which I have called them. So after they had fasted and prayed, they placed their hands on them and sent them off" (13:2–3). A praying church sent out its first missionaries.

In modern missions

While a student in Germany from 1710 to 1716, and an earnest follower of Christ, Count Zinzendorf with five other students formed the Order of the Grain of Mustard Seed, a society bound together with prayer. From this prayer group came the Moravian missionary movement, one of the most amazing missionary advances of that era. Many attribute their almost unapproachable record of missionary passion to their practice of unbroken intercession twenty-four hours a day, which continued for more than a hundred years. This may explain why one of every hundred Moravians became a foreign missionary. Zinzendorf's worldwide missionary movement is also credited with setting the stage for William Carey and the "Great Century" of missions that followed.

Dr. Harold Lindsell speaks of a German pastor by the name of Johannes Gossner (1773–1858). Gossner was a missionary enthusiast and a great prayer warrior. Lindsell reports, "During his lifetime, he was responsible for the sending out of one hundred and forty-four missionaries. A single sentence from his funeral message delivered before his open tomb tells eloquently what he did through prayer. 'He prayed up the walls of a hospital and the hearts of nurses; he prayed mission stations into being and missionaries into faith; he prayed open the hearts of the rich, and gold from the most distant lands.'"[2]

In the summer of 1806 a group of students from William College in Massachusetts met outdoors for prayer. A thunderstorm drove them under a haystack. Waiting for the storm to end, they prayed for an awakening of foreign missionary concern among their fellow students. Bowed in prayer, they volunteered themselves for foreign missionary service. That dedication gave birth to the first student missionary society in America. Adoniram Judson was one of those students. He and others of that group were the first Americans commissioned for service overseas.

Out of the 1859 revival in Britain came daily prayer meetings in Oxford and Cambridge with the undergraduates seeking "wholehearted consecration" to God. The prayer meetings continued unbroken for over a hundred years. The modern student movement of which InterVarsity is a part grew out of these prayer sessions. Also, hundreds of Christian leaders around the world owe their call to labor in God's work to their attendance at these prayer meeting in their student years.

One of the most graphic examples of laborers sent out through prayer comes from the life of Hudson Taylor, founder of the China Inland Mission. Onboard ship in 1874, he fell and injured his spine, necessitating a furlough and confinement to bed, which lasted for almost a year. This seemed a loss of time during which he could have been speaking in churches, stirring up interest in China. But God had a greater mission. Taylor had placed at the foot of his bed a large map of China. Laid aside, day after day he prayed that God would furnish money and workers to attack unreached inland provinces for the Kingdom.

Early in 1875 he sent to press a little paper, "Appeal for Prayer, on Behalf of More Than a Hundred and Fifty Million Chinese." He told of nine unopened provinces and asked friends of CIM to pray "that God will raise up this year 18 suitable men to devote themselves to this work." That year 18 candidates responded. Soon he had a class studying Chinese by his bed.

When he arrived in China around the start of 1877, he knew that political changes made it possible to enter all of China. Back in England at Christmas 1877, he asked workers and friends to pray with him for at least twenty-four men and six women in the following year. Twenty-eight new workers sailed before the end of the year. Several more were accepted before year-end who followed shortly after, putting the project over its goal.

In 1881 he estimated fifty or sixty new missionaries were immediately needed to help reach some of the multiplied millions. Then he thought that the number was too low. Remembering that the Lord appointed another seventy and sent them out, Taylor called a special prayer meeting and asked his fellow workers to petition God to send seventy new missionaries in the next three years. In 1883 several went but forty-six more were needed to complete the seventy. In 1884, the last of the three-year period, forty-six more sailed.

In 1887 he asked God for 100 new missionaries. Fervent prayer arose throughout both China and England for this number. Taylor said, "If you showed me a photograph of the whole hundred taken in China, I could not be more sure than I am now." Before the year was over, more than 600 had offered themselves. After careful evaluation 102 were finally selected. By December 8, 88 had left. By December 29, fourteen more had sailed, totaling 102.

In 1912 Dr. Samuel Zwemer accepted a call to relocate from his post in Arabia to Egypt to coordinate the missionary work for several boards to the entire Islamic world. During his first year in Cairo he was joined by William Borden, a Yale graduate who had volunteered for missionary service as a result of Zwemer's preaching. Though born into wealth and heir to the vast Borden fortune, Borden gave thousands of dollars to

Christian enterprises, denied himself many luxuries, and eagerly handed out tracts as he rode his bike through the steaming Cairo streets. After four months in Cairo, Borden died of spinal meningitis. On April 10, 1916, Dr. Zwemer met with a group of Christians in the New York home of Borden's mother to pray that God would send someone to take the place of her son whose ultimate goal had been to reach the Muslims of China. In Chicago, a young man named George K. Harris received the conviction that God was calling him to work among the Muslims of China. He obeyed and became a strong witness in China and Southeast Asia. Not till later did he learn of this prayer meeting, and that the day of his call to China came at the very time of the prayer meeting in New York for a laborer to take Borden's place.

Missionary executive Ray Buker Jr. commented that missionary interest at Wheaton College reached its high when Jim Elliot, later martyred by the Auca Indians, was president of the Foreign Missions Fellowship. He gives the reason, "Students were assigned to pray for every floor of students in each dorm. When missions interest was lacking on a floor, prayers were concentrated until the missionary fire was rekindled."

The chairman of a church missionary committee began a meeting by saying, "Let's make it a special request tonight to ask that more of our young people will respond to the missionary call. We do have some who have gone, but let's pray for more." In the next few years several young people became involved in missionary service, including the chairman's own daughter, who was accepted as a candidate by a mission society, did some deputation work, and raised considerable support before circumstances kept her home. The daughter of another committee member served several years in Cameroon under Wycliffe.

Some prayer warriors pray for candidates to go out under a specific board and to a particular field. In the '40s Marjorie Shelley was attending Northern Baptist Seminary when she applied for missionary service under a Baptist board. A few months later she was speaking in a Chicago church when a prominent local pastor struck up a conversation with her. He told her that he had heard her speak a few months before when she was a candidate under another board, and not headed for the Belgian Congo. Then he added, "You're going under the Conservative Baptist Foreign Mission board now, and to the Belgian Congo, aren't you?"

She said, "Yes, and to take Edna Mae Sill's place!"

He replied, "When I first saw you a few months ago, you looked so much like Edna Mae Sill that I began to pray to the Lord that He would change your mind and send you to take her place. And now I learn that God has answered prayer!"

Prayer for the Quality of the Labor Force

Once additional workers join the Lord's labor force, they still need our prayers to face the problems cropping up in their ministries. So we should not only pray for an increased quantity of laborers, but also for an improved quality of life and service. Here are some areas.

For Safety

Missionaries frequently find themselves in danger of banditry, kidnapping, and local warfare. Often they have been delivered through faithful prayer partners at home. A missionary pilot in Africa told me how one evening just before sunset, after flying blindly over clouds, a hole suddenly opened to reveal a rarely used airstrip on which he safely landed. On his next furlough, a lady in a supporting church informed him that she had felt an urgency to pray for him on a certain morning, which turned out to be the same day and exact hour he landed his plane.

A missionary and his national helpers were forced to camp on a hill one night. Carrying a significant amount of money, they were fearful of an attack by bandits, but prayed and went to sleep. Months later, a brigand chief came to the mission station for medical treatment. He asked the missionary if he had soldiers who guarded him that night. "We intended to rob you," he said, "but we were afraid of the twenty-seven soldiers." When the missionary told the story in the homeland, someone said, "We had a prayer meeting that night, and there were just twenty-seven of us present."

For Health

When V. Raymond Edman was a missionary in Ecuador, he became so ill that the doctor advised his wife to dye her wedding dress black for his anticipated funeral. Thousands of miles away in Boston his friend, Dr. Joseph Evans, unaware of Edman's illness, felt burdened to have his prayer group pray for Edman. They prayed earnestly. Edman recovered to go on for forty more years of remarkable service, many as President of Wheaton College.

For Power

Unless a missionary enjoys spiritual victory in his or her own life, they will eventually fail. Prayer brings power to one's ministry. We need to pray they will have doors of opportunity, boldness to speak, willingness to suffer, and courage to keep on. William Carey, the steady "father of modern missions," had a paralyzed, bedridden sister who prayed for him for fifty years.

This principle works for laborers at home. When Charles Haddon Spurgeon was approached by a delegation of pastors seeking the secret of his success, he took them down to his Metropolitan Tabernacle basement to show them his "power plant." There on their knees were three hundred people, praying for the service.

A major reason for Billy Graham's success is the millions of people who pray for him and his crusades. One prayer supporter says, "You can stand beside Billy Graham each time he steps before the microphone to face a waiting crowd. For years I have prayed for him daily, and at times feel I am standing right by him as he preaches the gospel to the thousands."

A missionary who had ten preaching stations asked ten supporting churches to choose a station and pray for it especially. Seven of the preaching points produced much fruit, but three were unproductive. A visit on his next furlough revealed the reason. Seven churches were faithful to their promise to pray; the other three were negligent.

For God's Choice of Leaders

In 1962 Billy Graham was looking for an executive director for the Billy Graham Evangelistic Association. One afternoon, needing a nap, Graham asked T. W. Wilson, one of his associate evangelists, to handle a handful of small tasks. A well-organized man, Wilson completed the list before Graham awoke. Graham was amazed. Wilson replied, "You wanted them done, didn't you? Well, I did them." Graham knew he had his man. He prayed about it, and around 2 a.m. the next morning went to Wilson's room, and awaking him, said, "I want you to come with me and help me." The sleepy Wilson objected. Graham reasoned with him and asked him to pray about it. Wilson said he didn't need to pray, for his mind was made up. But he was unable to sleep the rest of that night nor the next night. Realizing the Lord was impressing on him that he ought to go with Graham, he yielded. Since 1962 T. W. Wilson has spent most of his life at Billy Graham's side, serving as "his gatekeeper, travel agent, valet, nurse, adviser, buffer, booster, defender, listener, mine sweeper, and constant chaperon."[3]

Many believe that we need to be much in prayer over the crucial need for leaders in our western evangelical world. Numerous parachurch organizations with global ministries are led by older men who will leave the scene in a few short years. As generations come and go, the need for capable, godly leaders will always be with us.

A survey of fifty-five North American Protestant agencies listed the following problems missionaries most frequently face: relationships with other missionaries, cultural adjustment, stress management, raising children, marital difficulties, money pressures, loneliness. Missionaries should be honest in their communication with supporters on the home front so that intelligent prayer can be offered in their behalf.

Over two thousand Wheaton College alumni serve as missionaries in eighty-five countries. How does the college keep track of these worldwide ambassadors? In 1988 Wheaton Alumni Association came up with the Missionary Prayer Project. More than two hundred missionaries regularly send their prayer letters which are read, distilled, and then distributed to the Alumni board and to various members of the college community. The Alumni office staff pray for these specific requests during office devotions on Tuesday mornings. Many letters attest to answers to prayer.

The Danger of Praying for Laborers

The winner of a race seemed to be muttering to himself as he ran the last lap. He explained to a bystander that he had been praying. Pointing to his feet, he said, "I was saying, 'You pick 'em up, Lord, and I'll put 'em down.'" Although asking for the Lord's help, the runner was also doing what he could to help answer his prayer. As a proverb says, "Pray for a good harvest, but keep on plowing." The one who prays for laborers places responsibility on himself to help answer his prayer.

The one who prays may end up going

Beware! When we start praying for the Lord to thrust forth laborers into the harvest, we may suddenly realize that He is calling US, facing US with the momentous possibility of leaving OUR home for a strange territory, perhaps a foreign field and the ensuing cultural shock.

When Jesus first urged His small band of followers to pray for harvesters, many never realized that they would be among those sent out and would find themselves as members of either the Twelve or the Seventy, and thus helping to answer their own prayers. Many a person has begun to pray for a particular mission field, and before long, has found himself or herself a worker on that very field, convicted by his or her own prayer.

The one who prays should do some giving

A person who prays for a new church building should dig down in his pocket to help pay for the new edifice. Similarly, the one who prays for additional workers in the Lord's harvest should contribute to the support of those new candidates. It takes considerable money to train, outfit, transport, and pay the modest salary and other needs of missionary families. Missionary executives find it frustrating and lamentable to have dedicated, qualified missionaries delayed months, even years, in their departure to some needy field because of lack of money.

The one who prays should continue in prayer

Missionaries invariably urge people to pray for them. We should read their letters to learn their needs. We should pray for their physical and spiritual welfare, for linguistic competence, for harmony with fellow workers, for fruit in their labors, for national workers, and for missionary societies. Prayer is the mightiest force available. It will open doors, break down walls, and release the power of the Holy Spirit without which the best-concocted programs of man are useless.

Parents who pray may be asked to send their children

Countless persons have become missionaries because of the prayers of their parents, like those of John G. Paton, missionary to the New Hebrides islands, who said to him, "When you were given to us, we laid you upon the altar, our first born, to be consecrated, if God saw fit, as a missionary of the Cross; and it has been our constant prayer that you might be prepared, qualified, and led to this very decision."

A poor, elderly mother in Scotland headed for a missionary society meeting where only contributing members were admitted. When the doorman found out that she was not a giver, he turned her away. Walking a little distance, she thought of her son who years before had gone as a missionary to Sierra Leone and whose body lay buried in West Africa. She retraced her steps and explained to the doorman, "You asked me if I was a contributor. I forgot. I gave my only boy, and he is buried out in Sierra Leone." The doorman doffed his cap, bowed graciously, and said, "Please come in." He led her to a front seat.

The importance of those who stay at home

Perhaps we should not make so strong a distinction between those who have gone to the mission field and those who, staying at home, have furthered the cause of missions through prayer, giving, and administrative acumen. C. Stacey Woods, with all plans made to go to India in 1934, stayed home to found and direct InterVarsity Fellowship, which sponsors the five-day, year-end Urbana Missionary Conference that attracts nearly 20,000 students from campuses across America. Dawson Trotman stayed home but he engineered an important outreach through his founding of the Navigators now spread throughout the globe. Bill Bright developed a vision through Campus Crusade, reaching into over 150 countries and protectorates.

The Danger of Not Praying for Laborers

A group of men in an Oriental tribe, whose lives had been changed from ferocity and murder to love and peace, approached a missionary with this question, "Why did it take so long for your message to reach our tribe?" The missionary had no answer.

Is it not a blot upon the church of Christ that at times workers cannot be found, not only for the foreign field, but for many tasks on the home front as well? And is not a major hindrance to missionary outreach the low spiritual morale of the harvester, due in part to our failure to pray? May not a lack of prayer be the underlying cause for the breakdown of health in the lives of many missionaries? And for the personality clashes and dissensions? And for financial hardships? And for closed doors? And for lack of fruit? Failure to pray is essentially a mandate against missions. When we don't pray, purses tighten, doors are shut, hearts remain unresponsive, and volunteers are scarce.

Dr. Roland Bingham, founder of the Sudan Interior Mission, told of a young missionary couple that left Toronto, Canada, years ago to go out to Nigeria. At first all went well. They learned the language. He began to preach. A church was established. But then, their little child died. Then the mother became sick, and another baby died. Finally, the mother herself died. The father came home, broken and unannounced.

Arriving in Toronto, he went to his home church's Wednesday evening prayer meeting and sat near the back through the service. At the end the pastor said, "Is there anything else before we dismiss?" As the missionary was about to raise his hand, the pastor pronounced the benediction. The missionary began to sob convulsively. Someone reached over and asked, "Friend, what's the matter?" Then catching a glimpse of his face, he exclaimed, "Why it's our missionary! Our missionary has come back! Don't you have something to say to us?"

When he gained control of himself, the missionary said, "I wasn't going to say anything, but I am now. The last time I saw you, you stood down at the railroad station. And you ran down the track after the train started, waving and shouting, 'I'll pray for you until Jesus comes.'"

The missionary continued, "I wondered why we learned the language so well. It was because you prayed for us. I wondered why the Lord blessed in the church so much but I know it was because you prayed. Then after a few years you lost interest in praying. I searched my heart, thinking sin in my life caused the loss of my family. I've nearly driven myself crazy to find out where I've sinned against God to bring such judgment on me. But now," he said, "I know. I've sat through this entire prayer service, and you've not once mentioned the name of your missionary."

Notes
1. Curtis C. Mitchell, *Praying Jesus' Way* (Grand Rapids: Revell, 1991), p. 100.
2. Harold Lindsell, *Missionary Principles and Practice* (Grand Rapids: Revell, 1955), p. 317.
3. William Martin, *A Prophet With Honor* (New York: William Morrow & Co., 1991), p. 289.

CHAPTER 4

Giving Thanks—For What?

After suffering through two difficult years, an early colony on the New England shore gathered a modest harvest, caught plenty of cod and venison, had substantial cabins for shelter, and had made friends with the Indians. But some leaders had doubts about the winter ahead, so they called a day of prayer and fasting.

The people gathered, heard a protracted prayer about human weakness, then a detailed confession by an elder for both his and the community's shortcomings. Others rose to list their errors. The meeting droned on till finally a little man strode up front, and said, "I must dissent. I've heard enough of sin and doom."

A gasp of surprise went through the room. The man continued, "I have fasted till my stomach rebelled. I have meditated on my sins till my mind was reeling. Now, I must lift my eyes in thanks, or not lift them at all."

The startled gasp changed to a sigh of relief as he went on. "I know we've had privations. We froze. We starved. Some died. But now we have a harvest, wood for our fires, meat for our eating, clothes for our nakedness. Why do we abase ourselves? Let's be done with whimpers and complaints! Let's lift our hearts and thank the good Lord for the things we have! And let us end this pointless fasting!"

A murmur filled the room. The more eloquent confessors looked crestfallen. Neighbor looking at neighbor broke out in smiles. The entire outlook had changed. Within an hour the fireplace was lit, meat was provided, and pots were simmering. Women cooked. Men brought planks to set up tables and benches. By sundown the day of fasting and mourning had become a day of feasting and merriment, as an atmosphere of thanksgiving saturated the settlement.

An abounding spirit of gratitude should fill all Christians. We should say with the psalmist, "Every day will I praise you" (145:2). Daniel gave thanks three times daily (Dan. 6:10). Paul makes much of thankfulness in his epistles, mentioning it six times in his short letter to the Colossians (1:3, 12; 2:7; 3:15–17; 4:2). He indicates that a thankful spirit reflects a Spirit-filled life (Eph. 5:18–20; Col. 3:15–16).

Jesus Christ, who possessed the Holy Spirit without measure, owned a thankful spirit. In addition to the unconscious ways in which His appreciation was evident for many natural blessings, like birds, flowers, grass, and little children, He expressed specific gratitude on several occasions. At the beginning of the book we listed twenty-four occasions when Jesus offered prayer. Noting that in two of these situations we are told of double thanks, for the loaves and then for the fish in the feeding of the four thousand, and for the bread and for the cup at the institution of the Lord's Supper. Assuming that He prayed for the loaves and fish separately at the feeding of the five thousand, and adding in the two other instances of Jesus' gratitude mentioned later in this chapter, we have a strong case for claiming that *one-third* (8) of Jesus' total (24) recorded prayers involved thanksgiving. For Jesus, it wasn't just asking for things—it was prayer and praise. Giving thanks is as much a part of prayer as asking.

If Jesus, the Lord of glory, made the effort to say thanks, how much more should finite humans cultivate appreciation. We should be thankful not only *for* Him but *like* Him. We have categorized His instances of gratitude into four areas.

Jesus Was Thankful for Food

A concert violinist friend of mine tells how some years ago, when a student at New York's Juilliard School of Music, she was invited to an outdoor picnic at the home of the president of a prestigious, eastern divinity school. Everyone sat down on the benches and started right in to eat. Commented my friend who had been raised in a strong Christian background, "I sat with open mouth in surprise, so accustomed was I to saying grace before meals. Yet here in my first contact with this prominent seminary, no one asked the blessing—despite the presence of dozens of ministerial students and their president. I almost stood up and prayed out loud, but wisely gave a silent thanks."

Some Christians today neglect to bow their heads at mealtime to thank God, even silently, for their food. Yet Jesus was not ashamed to bow before thousands and audibly voice His gratitude. One day, at the peak of His popularity, Jesus was thronged by the multitudes. To get relief He and the Twelve withdrew by boat across the Sea of Galilee from Capernaum to Bethsaida, about 10 miles away. Because the lake was small, it wasn't difficult for people to follow by shore and soon catch up. In those days people didn't work from 9 to 5. Many were bosses or part owners of small businesses, perhaps engaged in farming or fishing. Nothing prevented them from dropping their tasks and following the miracle worker, some in their own small boats, but most walking. One little boy after Sunday School described them as "the multitude that loafs and fishes."

As the day progressed, people were tired, hungry, and far from home and store. The disciples suggested Jesus dismiss the people so they could hunt for food. When Jesus asked Philip where the disciples could buy bread to feed the crowd, Philip calculated that eight months' wages wouldn't be enough to buy a bite for everyone there. But Andrew, with mustard-seed faith, told Jesus, "There is a lad here who has five barley loaves and two small fishes." Then to protect himself he added, "But what are they among so many?" Jesus, honoring Andrew's faith, said, "Have the people sit down." Then He took the loaves, and looking up to heaven, gave thanks, broke and gave them to His disciples, and the disciples to the multitude. The feeding of the five thousand is the only miracle recorded in all four Gospels, and all four Gospels mention the grace (Matt. 14:19; Mark 6:41; Luke 9:16; John 6:11). Sometimes the verb "give thanks" is used; sometimes the verb "bless" or "invoke a blessing on." How often before a meal is someone called on to give thanks or bless the food.

Of what did Jesus' grace consist? The content of His prayer may be gleaned from these two acts: the giving of thanks, and the blessing. To give thanks is to recognize gratefully God as the ultimate provider of our food. To bless is to invoke divine favor on the food so it will give the eater strength and health. When Jesus prayed before feeding the five thousand, He did at least these two things. He thanked His heavenly Father for the provision of the loaves and fishes, and asked that this provision might nourish the bodies of those now tired and weak. And because He was about to perform a miracle, He may well have implored the power of God to multiply the bread and fish. That day there was more than enough to rejuvenate the five thousand men plus women and children.

Sometime later, in the region of Decapolis, another large crowd of four thousand gathered. Since they had nothing to eat for three days, Jesus said, "If I send them home hungry, they will collapse on the way, because some of them have come a long distance." Somehow forgetting the previous miracle, the disciples answered, "But where in this remote place can anyone get enough to feed them?" Despite their slowness of heart, Jesus asked how many loaves and fish were available, then performed another miracle. Mark mentions that Jesus gave thanks twice, for both the bread and the fish (Matt. 15:36; Mark 8:6–7). Again, two different verbs are used, "give thanks" and "bless."

Early Christians adopted the habit of saying the blessing (Rom. 14:6; 1 Cor. 10:30). Meats were created by God "to be received with thanksgiving" (1 Tim. 4:3). When grace is said at meals today, the same two basic elements are present: thanksgiving to God, and asking His favor on the food "to the strengthening of our bodies." Saying the blessing, giving thanks, and saying grace are synonymous terms. A boy was invited for lunch to a neighbor's house, where the blessing was regularly asked. The boy was asked if he could say "grace." "Sure," he replied, "grace." He thought it was a girl's name, because grace was never offered by his parents.

Giving thanks for bread and fish encompasses a vast area of divine power. Tracing the history of the loaves takes us back to the fields where the grain grew and to the skies from which the showers dropped. Similarly, the fish lead us back to stream, river, and lake. Giving thanks envelops a wide, sweeping outlook including bounties of sky, sea, and earth.

On a visit to Haiti in 1980 to observe World Relief in action,

I shall never forget seeing 300 boys and girls, each served a hot bowl of food at noon recess in a school near Port au Prince. This was part of a quarter million dollar program which fed 15,000 children a meal five days a week. For some it was the only meal of the day. Nor shall I ever forget the grace they sang before they ate, "Merci, merci, merci" (Thanks, thanks, thanks).

The first Thanksgiving in America was celebrated in 1621 by the Pilgrims at Plymouth in gratitude for bountiful crops, following a year of struggle in which 47 of the 103 members of the colony died. Thanksgiving became an annual national holiday in 1863. In Quebec, Canada, in the early years inhabitants baked their bread in outdoor ovens. Until well into the nineteenth century the head of a family carved a cross on top of the unbaked loaf. Still on the golden crust after baking, this mark was the pious pioneers' way of thanking God for their daily bread.

In our blessed America the once-prevalent practice of saying grace is fast fading from the scene. One Christian whose duties took him coast to coast remarked that he had eaten in restaurants from New York to Los Angeles and could count on the fingers of one hand the number of people he had seen bow their heads in public, even to silently say grace. I recall bowing my head with two other preachers in a restaurant in Buffalo, New York, as a low-spoken thanks was offered. I also recall the waitress hurrying over to ask if anything was wrong with the food!

A trip abroad would soon enlighten Americans to their God blessed, bountiful supply of food. TV cameras have vividly highlighted the plight of thousands dying of hunger in Ethiopia and Somalia.

In a poor hill tribe in Columbia, South America, a new Christian could not understand the meaning of the New Testament word "gluttonous." Even after hearing it explained that a glutton was someone who eats excessively, he could scarcely grasp its significance, simply because he rarely ever had enough to satisfy his hunger.

In the '70s a mother in Canada, who had lived in England during the Second World War, was unhappy to hear her teenage daughter complain about the nutritional meals served at home. She decided to teach her daughter a lesson, so went to the library to check on what she as a girl had eaten during the London blitz.

Then she put her daughter on the same diet: a week's rations of
14 ounces of meat, 3 eggs, 2 pounds of potatoes, and 2 ounces
of cheese. For Sunday dinner the teenager was served bread and
butter and a hard-boiled egg. Said the daughter, "It was a good
lesson. I'll never complain again."

Often those who do want to say grace in public but not to
appear pious, will go through the motions quickly. One man
would rub his eyebrows. Another would bow his head for an
instant, flashing his hand across his forehead, as though bothered
by a fly or headache. One deacon's daughter, not wanting to be
ridiculed, would drop her fork, and stooping to pick it up, would
mumble, "God, bless the food, Amen."

A farmer, with the courage of his convictions, entered a city
restaurant, and quietly bowed his head when the food was served.
A young man at the next table, trying to embarrass him, called
out in a loud voice, "Hey, farmer, does everyone do that out in
the country where you live?" The farmer calmly replied, "No, son,
the pigs don't."

Some say grace twice at each meal. Some editions of the *English
Tudor*, an early school text in Great Britain similar to our *New
England Primer*, contain a prayer for after a meal in addition to
one before. Visiting a Missouri Lutheran home at lunchtime, I
was pleasantly surprised to hear the minister offer prayer, not only
before we started, but also after we had eaten.

Something about the way Jesus presided at dinners made an
indelible impression on His disciples. On the first Easter afternoon
the Lord encountered two discouraged disciples on the road to
Emmaus. Although He chatted with them for quite a while, they
failed to recognize Him until He sat down in their home to eat.
As He blessed the bread, and broke it, then "their eyes were
opened and they recognized him" (Luke 24:31).

Sixty years after Jesus fed the five thousand, the disciples could
not forget that Jesus had said grace before the meal. John, in his
Gospel, identified a place in Jesus' travels by mentioning the
thanks as well as the miracle. "Then some boats from Tiberias
landed near the place where the people had eaten the bread after
the Lord had given thanks" (John 6:23). The offering of thanks
loomed as memorable as the miracle itself. Gratitude for food
should be important to us, as it was to Jesus.

Jesus Was Thankful for the Spiritual Insight Given to the Simple

Many cities around Galilee were highly favored because of the ministry of the Seventy, sent out by Jesus to teach and with the power to cast out demons. Especially privileged was Capernaum where Jesus spent a large portion of His early ministry and performed several of His miracles. But many self-sufficient residents of these cities were blinded to Jesus' true nature. Jesus warned these people that they would be cast down from their exalted position and suffer greater condemnation than Sodom in the day of judgment (Luke 10:12–15).

Jesus was thankful that though the religious leaders and important people rejected His claims, many of the less sophisticated and social nobodies turned to Him to satisfy their spiritual needs because they understood who He really was. He said, "I praise you, Father, Lord of heaven and earth, because you have hidden these things from the wise and learned, and revealed them to little children. Yes, Father, for this was your good pleasure" (Luke 10:21; see also Matt. 11:25–26).

The word translated "praise" means literally "to make an open and full confession, to acknowledge." Verbal announcements and printed programs often carry acknowledgments expressing thanks to some benefactor. Translators are divided between "thank" and "praise." The above NIV verses read "praise" while the King James Version says "thank." The idea of Jesus' prayer is, "I fully recognize and rejoice and praise and thank You." Jesus gave thanks because His heavenly Father had revealed spiritual truth to the lowly, while hiding it from the clever.

The Lord did not mean that intellectual attainment blocked faith, but rather that it was unnecessary for true belief. Untutored persons can apprehend saving truth. Lack of learning does not disqualify. On the other hand, ignorance may have its advantage. Those who humbly realize their emptiness are more readily receptive to divine wisdom than those smugly filled with their own learning. Know-it-alls have little room for more knowledge. Perhaps we could paraphrase His words, "You don't have to be in *who's who* to know *what's what.*"

Jesus continually hid things from the wise skeptics and learned unbelievers, but revealed truth to His unpretentious, simple disciples. The Pharisees asked for a sign, but He gave them none except that of the prophet Jonah (Matt. 12:38 ff). However, when His disciples asked for a sign, His answer covered the space of two chapters (Matt. 24–25).

One reason Jesus spoke in parables was to continue the confusion of disbelievers. He told His disciples, "Because it is given unto you to know the mysteries of the kingdom of heaven, but to them it is not given. . . . Therefore speak I to them in parables; because they seeing see not; and hearing they hear not, neither do they understand" (Matt. 13:10–13). Later He proceeded to explain to the disciples privately the meaning of the parables He had uttered publicly.

If we puzzle as to why the God saw fit to enlighten the simple and confound the so-called wise, we point to the sovereign will of the Father. Jesus addressed this prayer to the "Lord of heaven and earth," the Sovereign of the universe, and ended it, "Yes, Father, for this was your good pleasure."

The proud Pharisees did not believe His deity, but this basic truth was revealed to simple Peter (Matt. 16:16–18).

When Jesus healed a forty-year-old man born blind, the Pharisees would not accept this miracle, despite the evidence. Jesus commented, "For judgment I have come into this world, so that the blind will see and those who see will become blind" (John 9:39). The blind man saw both physically and spiritually. But the Pharisees, who claimed to have the light, were really blind—spiritually blind.

Those who did not wish to know the truth received no light from the Lord. When Jesus was sent by Pilate to Herod's jurisdiction, Herod hoped Jesus would perform some miracle. But Jesus did no miracle to satisfy the whim of an unbeliever who wished to degrade Jesus to the level of a magician (Luke 23:8).

After the resurrection He did not appear to unbelievers like Pilate, Annas, Caiaphas, the Sadducees, or the Pharisees. He knew they would be unconvinced, even by a personal appearance. But He did show Himself to His followers over and over again.

Paul described the members of the early church not too complimentarily. "Not many of you were wise by human standards; not many were influential; not many were of noble birth" (1 Cor. 1:26). Not many of the intellectuals like Gamaliel, not many of the influential like Felix or Festus, not many of the illustrious like Agrippa or Nero, were found in evangelical ranks. Rather they were ordinary people, the "hoi polloi," not from the ranks of the "four hundred" or "bluebloods," instead, often unschooled, social zeros, described by second-century historian Celsus as "wool-workers, cobblers, leather-dressers and the most clownish of men," who constituted the major segment of the church. In his massive church history, Latourette of Yale points out that in India by far the majority of early converts came from the lower castes, in some areas almost exclusively.

But it doesn't say not ANY wise men. Lady Huntingdon, a woman of wealth and social status, and patron of both Wesley and Whitefield, used to say she was saved by an "m" for if it had said ANY instead of MANY, she could not have been redeemed. Through the centuries some of the intelligentsia like Pascal, Bacon, Wilberforce, and Disraeli, have believed. But they have always been a minority. As a rule, spiritual truth has been revealed to the unimportant and hidden from VIPs.

It's possible to know all about rocks but not to know the Rock of Ages; to know all about flowers but not to be acquainted with the Rose of Sharon and the Lily of the Valley; to understand much about light but not to follow the Light of the world; to comprehend the stars and trace the planets in their courses but not to know the Bright and Morning Star; to grasp the major philosophies of the world but not to accept Him who is the Truth and the key to the rational explanation of the universe.

How wonderful when the elite are also believers in divine revelation. The initial moon landing was made by Neil Armstrong and Buzz Aldrin on July 20, 1969. In a book twenty years later, *Men From Earth*, Aldrin describes a not too widely publicized incident that occurred soon after the two astronauts in the lunar module Eagle landed on the moon's Sea of Tranquility. Aldrin, a "religious" man, wishing to give thanks for a safe moon landing, had been forbidden to do so. Too many complaints had been received when a former Apollo crew the previous Christmas Eve had read verses from Genesis over the air while orbiting the moon, and NASA wanted no more confrontations with antireligious groups. So before taking those first uncertain steps on the moon's surface, Aldrin asked for a moment of silence, opened a small

Communion kit prepared by his Presbyterian pastor, and poured wine from a vial about the size of the tip of his little finger into a tiny chalice. Before going back on the air, he ate a tiny piece of bread, swallowed the wine, and silently gave thanks for the intelligence and spirit that had brought two young pilots to the Sea of Tranquillity.[1]

Jesus Was Thankful for Answered Prayer

Probably Jesus' greatest miracle was the raising of Lazarus from the dead after four days in the grave. Lazarus sickened and died while Jesus was out of the area. His sisters, Martha and Mary, sent for Him, but He came too late, at least in their opinion. Both lamented, "If You had been here, my brother would not have died." Jesus asked to see the burial site.

At the grave the humanity and deity of Jesus blended beautifully. Jesus wept in genuine sorrow at the loss of a beloved friend. While tears were trickling down His holy cheeks, He cried with the voice of power, "Lazarus, come forth!" Between these demonstrations of manhood and Godhood, before raising Lazarus, Jesus lifted His eyes to heaven and said, "Father, I thank you that you have heard me. I knew that you always hear me" (John 11:41–42). Jesus was thankful for a petition-hearing and a prayer-answering Father.

But there was more to His prayer. Jesus prayed aloud so that His hearers might understand that, when in a few minutes Lazarus shuffled forth from the grave bound hand and foot, they would be witnesses to a mighty, powerful work of God, attesting the divine source of Jesus' person and message. Jesus was putting His credibility on the line by praying out loud for the resurrection of Lazarus. Everyone heard Him. Who can bring anyone back from the dead? And in the grave four days? Jesus was praying, in effect, "If I raise Lazarus, certainly they will recognize Me as God's Son. If Lazarus does not rise, let Me be acclaimed as an impostor." Jesus called on His Father to answer His prayer so that the Father might be acknowledged as the Sender of His Son, and Jesus as the One sent. Many did believe.

Jesus was thankful for answered prayer, which was no exception for Him, but a repeated happening. "You always hear Me," He prayed. The Lord wishes us to delight in the regular experience of answered prayer. Most answers fall in the routine, ordinary category, but some come with speed and drama.

When a plant closed down on Long Island, an electronics engineer was unable to find work. He sent his resumé to company after company, but without success. Too proud to tell relatives of their financial status, the couple were down to their last can of noodle soup.

As was their custom, they bowed their heads to pray the Lord's Prayer. The husband loved to eat bread with soup but today there was no bread. With deliberate emphasis the couple intoned, "Give us this day our daily bread."

Just then came a firm, insistent knocking at the back door. They hurried through the rest of the prayer; then the wife answered the door. The husband heard a neighbor say, "Can you use any bread? My brother is a route man for a big company. They're having an advertising campaign, giving out sample loaves. He was given more than he needed for his stores. He has four cases left. He can't bring the cases back because the bread has to be fresh each day. I've taken two cases and can't fit any more in my house. Can you use the other two?" Husband and wife were astonished at how quickly and sufficiently their prayer was answered—and most thankful.

Many Psalms are thanksgivings to God for answers to prayer. When the Lord rescued David from the hand of King Saul, David broke forth in praise, ending, "Therefore I will praise you among the nations, O LORD" (Ps. 18:49). When Paul was delivered from deadly peril through the prayers of caring friends, many thanks were given to the Lord because of his escape (2 Cor. 1:11). Thankfulness for answered prayer reflects the glory of God.

One summer evening in southeast England during the dark days of World War II, a pastor walked into his church and was surprised to find a little boy kneeling near the front. After questioning, the lad explained, "You see—I was afraid my father would be left on the beach at Dunkirk, so I prayed every day for him. Now that he's home safe, I've come to give thanks." It's so easy to forget to say thanks. But this little boy modeled Jesus who said, "Father, I thank You that You have heard Me."

Ken Taylor, publisher of *The Living Bible*, traces the

development of his prayer practices through the years. Though prayer had always been significant to him, it was in seminary when prayer and daily devotional Bible reading became of utmost importance. He began to rise at 5 instead of 6 a.m. for Scripture reading and prayer. Someone told him about the value of writing down on an index card the items that should be remembered in prayer, then checking them off when the answers came. He says it was a great joy to be able to cross off the answered petitions. But he has long since found an advanced step which enhances his prayer life considerably. "Now," he says, "instead of immediately crossing off the answered item, I put a check mark beside it, and for several days take time to give thanks before going on to other items.[2]

Jesus Was Thankful for His Own Sacrifice on the Cross

The night before His death Jesus celebrated Passover with His disciples. The Gospels state that at this time He instituted the ordinance known as the Lord's Supper during which He gave thanks twice, before both breaking the bread and drinking the cup (Matt. 26:26–27; Mark 14:22–23; Luke 22:19–20). These elements symbolized His crucified body and His shed blood. The night before He died, with full knowledge of His imminent sacrifice for sin, He gave thanks for His redemptive death.

In relating how the Lord's Supper was initiated, information which he received by direct revelation from the Lord, Paul specifically mentions the giving of thanks by Jesus before each element (1 Cor. 11:23–25). So vital a part does thanksgiving play in this ordinance that Greek, Latin, and Oriental churches call it the "Eucharist," which means "the giving of thanks."

That night Jesus knew fully the significance of the broken bread and of the wine. His body would be wounded and bruised because of our iniquities. His blood would be shed for the forgiveness of our sins. The moment for which He had been born was upon Him. All the agonies He would experience in those awesome hours on the cross were pictured by the bread and wine. Though the shadow of death was over Him, He thanked God—a vivid example of giving "thanks in all circumstances" (1 Thes. 5:18).

In Old Testament times lambs and bulls came bleating and

bellowing to the brazen altar to be sacrificed. But the true Lamb of God opened not His mouth except to give thanks.

A painting of the sufferings of Jesus changed the direction of German Count Zinzendorf's life, and set him on a course which eventually earned him the title of the "Father of Moravian missions." At age nineteen, on a tour of Germany, he visited an art gallery in Dusseldorf.

Among all the masterpieces the one that left its mark on him was a painting, Domenico Feti's *Ecce Homo*, that depicted Jesus enduring the crown of thorns. Beneath was a Latin inscription, "This I have suffered for you, but what have you done for Me?" Zinzendorf thought that he had done very little, and knew that he could never be happy living the life of a nobleman. No matter the cost, he would seek a life of service for the Savior who had suffered so much to save him.

During World War II, Frank Gajowniczek, a sergeant in the Polish Army, was captured by the Nazis and sent to the German concentration camp at Auschwitz. In July 1941, some prisoners escaped. In retaliation the Nazis arbitrarily selected ten innocent victims who were sentenced to death by starvation. An eyewitness described what happened.

"Among the ten chosen was Gajowniczek. Immediately he cried out, 'Have mercy! I have a wife and children! I don't want to die! I want to live to see them!'

A moment later a man stepped forward. He was a priest, Maximillian Kolbe, who had been captured by the Gestapo a few months before and brought to Auschwitz. He told the commandant that he was willing to take the place of the man who had a family." The commandant, surprised at such compassion, permitted the exchange. The priest joined the other nine and endured the terrible suffering from hunger for two weeks before they gave him a deadly injection. The soldier was eventually released to rejoin his wife and children.

When I read this story back in the late seventies, Sergeant Gajowniczek had made a yearly pilgrimage without fail to Auschwitz and placed a wreath on Father Kolbe's grave to remind him of the man who died in his place.

Have you ever made a pilgrimage to the Cross and beheld One hanging there for you, dying in your place, not just so you could live another few years on this earth, but so you could live forever?

Notes
1. Fred Howard, review of *Men From Earth* by Buzz Aldrin and Malcolm McConnell, *New York Times* (2 July 1989).
2. Ken Taylor with Virginia Muir, *My Life: A Guided Tour* (Wheaton: Tyndale, 1991,) p. 348.

CHAPTER 5

Facing Crisis

Ten years married, sports figure Pat Williams faced a crisis in his relationship with his wife, Jill, a former runner-up to the Miss Illinois 1972 title. It was a Sunday, and the bomb broke after the family returned from the morning service. Jill had been giving him the silent treatment after an earlier remark, and he knew that he had some fence-mending to do. He tried to find out exactly what had offended her, but she remained sullen, replying, "Nothing." Pat said, "Something's been bothering you and we're going to sit here and get this straightened out if it takes all day."

Jill hadn't planned to say what she then said. "I just don't care anymore. I hate this marriage. It's boring me to death." Then she listed a dozen charges, like "You never share anything with me, your work, your Bible study, your dreams. You never act as if I were important to you in front of people. Don't give me crumbs. I want the real thing. I want you."

Pat could hardly sleep that night. His well-ordered world as an NBA manager of such teams as the Chicago Bulls, the Atlanta Hawks, and now the Philadelphia 76ers, was coming apart. Where had he failed? Coming home after work next day, he found Jill, face expressionless and emotionally dead. He had been reading a new book by Chuck Swindoll, and was haunted by this sentence, "For God to do an impossible work, He must take an impossible man and crush him." It was near midnight when he surrendered to the Lord in total honesty. In tears he cried out, "Lord, do to me whatever you have to. I've got a crisis here that obviously I have caused. Crush me. Show me. Help me." The story of how the marriage was restored after a long struggle is grippingly told in their book *Rekindled.* Pat had a crisis and prayed.[1]

Jesus prayed at times of crisis. Though He never suffered any problem due to His own shortcomings, for He was without sin, He was nevertheless confronted by several critical situations. When an emergency arose, His first reaction was to pray. How unlike most of us who frequently make prayer our last recourse.

Jesus was not like a "foxhole Christian" praying only in a time of danger and as a last resort. Prayer was a regular, daily practice. But whenever tough occasions confronted Him, He went to prayer. Emergencies were overcome through consultation with His heavenly Father. Fresh crises prompted fresh calls to prayer. His example fits the saying, "We can do more than pray, but not until after we have prayed."

The emergency number 911 may get tied up. But the Lord's line is never too busy to hear our plea for help. Someone wrote,

> I wait in long lines wherever I go.
> On the phone "please hold" seems ten minutes or so.
> As I simmer at red lights, my patience slow leaks.
> For appointments I'm told, "We're booked solid for weeks."
> Yet the God of my life stands in wait for my call—
> When I need an appointment there is no wait at all.

The National Weather service advises anyone caught in the open during a severe lightning storm to kneel down, bend forward, and put hands on knees. Should lightning strike nearby, one's body would be less likely to serve as a conductor. Likewise, in times of spiritual danger, protection comes from a kneeling posture. In crises Jesus went to prayer.

This chapter deals with some of these emergencies, while other crises are handled elsewhere in this book, such as the dilemma of whom to choose as apostles (chapter 3) and the struggle in Gethsemane (chapter 9).

At the Attempt to Make Him King
After He Fed the Five Thousand

Immediately after feeding the five thousand, "Jesus made his disciples get into the boat and go on ahead of him to Bethsaida, while he dismissed the crowd. After leaving them, he went up on a mountainside to pray" (Mark 6:45–46; see also Matt. 14:23).

It was probably time for His evening prayer. The multitudes were beginning to intrude on His quiet hour. More than that, they displayed intentions of making Him king by force. So Jesus first compelled His disciples to get into the boat and sail to the other side. Then He sent the crowds away, ascended the high tableland at the foot of which the five thousand had been fed, and when evening came, He was there alone. Jesus virtually had to force the disciples into the boat, perhaps because they wished to be with Him if the crowd was going to organize a coronation ceremony. Or maybe they sensed a storm, and didn't think it a good night to cross the lake. Did Jesus have to give the boat a shove to start them on their way? He knew that struggling in a storm would be less dangerous for the disciples than staying with the wrong crowd who wanted to make Him an earthly king.

Jesus was on the mountain (colloquial for hill country) a long time. Suppose it was as late as 9 p.m. when He ordered His disciples into the boat. It wasn't till the fourth watch (between 3 and 6 a.m.) that He came walking on the water to rescue them. This was certainly a protracted period. One commentator thinks it was eight hours. What did He pray about during those hours?

Certainly He felt the need of recharging His spiritual batteries after all the long hours of teaching that day, and after expending the miraculous force to multiply the loaves and fish. Where did He get the power to perform wonders? Where would He get the healing balm for tomorrow's miracles? Where He always received it—in the place of prayer.

He also knew that the disciples were going to be hit by a raging tempest. Though several were seasoned sailors who made their livelihood on the sea and knew how to handle a boat in rough waters, this night they would find themselves in grave trouble as the waves tossed their craft like a piece of cork. As the fierce storm continued unabated, they might think that He had forgotten them. But He was watching over them. As they kept bucking the headwinds amid darkness and billows, they wondered where He was. In His omniscience He could see them struggling wearily at the oars. Later, at the proper moment, He would come walking on the water and still the storm, but in the meantime He was praying for them. This reminds us, when the storms of life roar about us, that the eye of the Omnipotent who holds the whole world in His hand is watching over us.

Though He prayed for the renewal of His personal resources and for the safety of the Twelve in the storm, His major reason for praying that night is given in John: "Jesus, knowing that they intended to come and make him king by force, withdrew again to a mountain by himself" (6:15).

Crowds had become a problem for Jesus. Once the crush in front of a house was so great that to reach Jesus a paralytic man had to be lowered through a roof. Day after day, wave after wave of needy people jostled Him. On one occasion, because of the physical danger of a pressing throng, He ordered His disciples to ready a getaway boat (Mark 3:9). Often masses prevented Him from eating, or forced Him to take refuge in a house. Jesus was now at the peak of His popularity. By the thousands they came, exhilarated by idle curiosity, by the love of excitement, but mostly by the performance of amazing deeds. Three verbs in John 6:2 are in the imperfect tense, indicating continuous action. The verse reads literally, "A great multitude *was following* Him because they *were seeing* His miracles which He *was doing.*" And now He had just electrified the populace by feeding five thousand with a few loaves and fish. The politician who provides or even promises a prosperous economy usually gains popularity. Jesus now had their vote. They wanted to make Him king forcibly.

Jesus faced a test. He had come to die, ultimately to be king. Now they were offering Him the crown apart from the Cross. By acceding to their wish, He could mount the throne without the suffering of Calvary. He saw the pitfall, and felt the need of getting alone in prayer in order to refocus on His mission, brush aside the superficiality of their allegiance, and renew the strength to follow the ordained path. To get alone with His Father, He excused His disciples, expelled the mob, climbed the heights, and poured out His heart. The crisis called for prayer.

Prayer strengthened His resolve not to be dazzled by the popularity. He knew that much of the populace had missed the import of the miracle. Instead of pondering the nature and authority of the person who could feed so many with so little, they were seeking to make Him king because they saw Him as one who could supply their daily bread and heal their ills. They were grasping at the physical goodies but not bowing to His spiritual claims. He knew that later when they began to understand His demands, many would turn away and follow Him no more. He reminded Himself that He had come to give His life a ransom for many, and that He could not bypass the Cross. It was the Cross that would lead to the throne. He knew the attempt to make Him king was political dynamite which would sabotage the purpose for which He had come. His strengthened resolve was evident the next day when the same crowd found Him on the other side of the lake, and engaged Him in dialogue. In His discourse He claimed to be the Bread of Life sent from heaven. "On hearing it, many of his disciples said, 'This is a hard teaching. Who can accept it?'" (John 6:60). "From this time many of his disciples turned back and no longer followed him" (v. 66).

What an example to all who are tempted by human honors! We need to exercise humility, deny illegitimate ambition even though it may cost us the plaudits of people, and realize that God will not give His honor to another.

A Vermont farmer lost his valuable watch in his barn. Loudly lamenting his misfortune, he took his flashlight and raked the sawdust on the floor, but in vain. Hired help, motivated by the offer of a reward, also joined the search. But all the noisy searching failed to turn up the watch. When the men left for lunch, a small boy slipped quietly into the barn and found the watch. Asked by the astonished farmer how he had discovered it, the lad replied, "I just laid down on the sawdust, kept very still, and soon I heard the watch ticking."

In times of stress we need to draw aside from the noise of the crowd and listen for the sound of God's voice.

Before Giving Disturbing News to the Twelve

Another crisis arose well into the final year of Jesus' ministry. The opposition of religious leaders was intensifying. His popularity with the common people, though still strong, was beginning to diminish. Many professing followers were deserting His ranks, claiming His teachings were hard. Planning to get alone with the Twelve to instruct them more deeply, He wondered if they had grasped who He really was. What did they think of Him? And when He did tell them of His imminent sufferings, how would they react? Would they be ready for this disturbing news?

To prepare them for this momentous announcement of His coming death, Jesus took the Twelve aside to a solitary place away from the crowds where He engaged in a session of prayer. Though the disciples were present, He alone was praying. Then He put a question to them. Luke states the situation thus: "Once when Jesus was praying in private and his disciples were with him, he asked them, 'Who do the crowds say I am?' They replied, 'Some say John the Baptist; others say Elijah; and still others, that one of the prophets of long ago has come back to life.' 'But what about you?' he asked. 'Who do you say I am?' Peter answered, 'The Christ of God'" (Luke 9:18–20). Jesus declared that Peter's affirmation came not through human discovery but through divine revelation, and announced a high honor for Peter—he would be given a leading role in the founding of the church.

Then Jesus broke the distressing news. He began to predict His coming sufferings, His rejection by the religious leaders, His death at Jerusalem, and His rising from the dead on the third day. Peter began to rebuke Jesus, strongly denying such things would ever happen. In his mind Peter pictured Jesus victorious and seated on a throne, not dying ignominiously on a cross. Although the Old Testament foresaw a Messiah who would suffer as well as reign, most Messianic expectations dwelt on His glorious kingdom. Peter would spare his Master the sufferings. Peter was gloriously correct on the person of Christ, but tragically wrong on the work of Christ. He had just been congratulated as the recipient of a revelation from God the Father. Now he was called a tool of the devil. Jesus said, "Get behind me, Satan" (Matt. 16:23). Why was commendation so soon followed by condemnation?

It was Peter's denial of Jesus' sufferings that drew such a strong reaction. Jesus said, in effect, "Peter, don't you see that you are cutting out the core of the gospel? To forgive sins I must die.

Without the shedding of blood there is no remission. The path to the kingdom is by way of the Cross. Without My death there will be no dominion. Don't you realize it's the Devil who is prompting you to deny the Cross? Peter, you are repeating the same temptation I suffered from the Devil when he offered me all the kingdoms of the world. If no Cross, all will be loss. Peter, you are not minding the things of God, but of men!"

"Then Jesus said to them all, 'If anyone would come after me, he must deny himself and take up his cross daily and follow me. For whoever wants to save his life will lose it, but whoever loses his life for me will save it'" (Luke 9:23–24). Not only was Jesus determined to follow the path of suffering and death undeterred by Peter's passionate objection, but He was insisting that the apostles must have the same willingness to sacrifice their lives.

This disturbing news would be a tough dose for the Twelve to swallow. F. L. Godet suggests that Jesus, anticipating the impression such news would have on them, prepared Himself for this important step by prayer.[2] His prayer was answered. According to strong tradition, except for Judas everyone of the Twelve laid down his life for the Gospel.

At the Visit of the Greeks

The episode of a delegation of Greeks who wanted to see Jesus during Passion week in Jerusalem has been called Jesus' second great temptation, the first being His temptation by the Devil right after His baptism at the start of His ministry.

Apparently the Greeks were attempting to enlist Jesus as their teacher. Greek philosophy had failed to satisfy their deepest needs. Hearing of Jesus' wisdom, they wished to engage His services. This was a powerful temptation—an appealing assignment. But it had a catch, the same as in the attempt to make Him king. He had come, not only to instruct, but by dying to give His life a ransom for many. His divine schedule called for His death on the cross in about four days.

Viewing the Greeks, He immediately referred to His "hour," an unmistakable allusion to the Cross and its accompanying events. He gave the analogy of wheat. Unless a kernel falls into the ground and dies, it remains but a single seed. But if it dies, it produces many seeds. Was it not momentarily enticing to think of turning away from the scourging and the nails to become a teacher of the Greeks, and not to die? Naturally, He shrank from the cross, but we must not confuse any possible fleeting reaction with His basic determination to fulfill His mission by sacrificing Himself.

Facing this temptation to lure Him from His prescribed path, He prayed, "Now my heart is troubled, and what shall I say? 'Father, save me from this hour'? No, it was for this very reason I came to this hour. Father, glorify your name!" (John 12:27–28).

Note that Jesus is not asking to escape the cross, but rather is asking a question, "Should I ask to be saved from this hour? No! That would not be proper, for this is the specific purpose for which I came to earth in the first place." To set His face unflinchingly toward the cross, offer Himself thereon as a ransom for sin, be buried and rise the third day would bring glory to His Father's name. At the end of His prayer came a voice from heaven, "I have glorified it, and will glorify it again" (12:28b).

The people standing by, hearing the voice but unable to distinguish the words, thought it had thundered, or was the voice of an angel. The phenomenon confirmed the Father's approval of the Son's request. Perhaps later, some of the bystanders would realize the supreme importance of Jesus' death.

It should be noted that this prayer was not offered off in some solitary spot, but in a crowd. In time of crisis when Jesus had no time to withdraw to a quiet haunt, He confronted the problem immediately by sending up an SOS to His Father.

As pointed out in chapter 1, the Father's voice was heard three times during Jesus' ministry, and each time Jesus was praying. First at the beginning at His baptism. Second, in the middle, at His transfiguration. And third, on this occasion, a few days before the cross. And all three occasions pointed to His death. Jesus had come to die, and He resisted every attempt to divert Him from the cross.

Ida Scudder, born in India in 1870 to missionary parents, returned to the United States for her schooling. She had no intention of following the family tradition and becoming a missionary. But soon after her graduation from D. L. Moody's school for girls at Northfield, Massachusetts, an urgent cablegram informing her of her mother's serious illness brought her back to India. She planned only to help her mother back to health, then leave that "horrible country, with its heat, dust, noise, and smells" and return to America to be with all her friends, and to pursue her own ambitions.

Ida's stay in India grew longer than planned. Besides the care of her mother, other tasks needed to be done, like teaching in a girls' school and helping her physician-missionary father. Though happy to be reunited with her family, she felt uncomfortable from the pressure of family members to become a missionary. Ida wasn't keen on assuming the burdens of missionary life. It took an unusual incident to convince her.

On the same night three different men, a Brahmin, a highcaste Hindu, and a Muslim, all came to her door, begging for help in difficult childbirths. Religious convention prohibited these women from having close contact with male strangers, which meant refusal of her father-doctor's assistance. Ida could not sleep that night. Three women were dying, and she couldn't help them because she was untrained. But she did not wish to spend her life in India. Her friends were urging her to return to the pleasant life and wonderful opportunities of America. Confronted with this crisis, she prayed a long time for guidance before going to bed. She said, "I think that was the first time I ever met God face to face, and all that time it seemed that He was calling me into this work." Early in the morning she heard the tom-tom beating in the village, the signal that someone had died. Soon she learned that all three women had died during the night. Again she shut herself in her room. After much prayer she went to her parents and told them she had to return to America to study medicine, and to come back to help these women. She returned to India after graduating from Cornell Medical College.

When she died in 1960 at age ninety, she had seen a one-room dispensary with a few patients grow into a modern medical complex with nearly 100 doctors, a 484-bed general hospital, a 60-bed eye hospital, plus numerous mobile clinics, serving 200,000 patients and training 200 medical students each year. She was so famous that a letter simply addressed, "Dr. Ida, India," arriving on the continent, was directed immediately to her hospital.

When Confronting the Impossible

We are specifically told that Jesus prayed before performing some of His miracles. Likely, He prayed before all of them.

One purpose of Jesus' miracles was to declare the ultimate triumph of God's kingdom over Satan and all His cohorts of evil. Every time Jesus performed a miracle, He faced all the reality and power of the devil. In the weakness of His humanity He needed divine strength. So He prayed for power.

Before Jesus healed *a deaf and mute man* in the region of the Decapolis, He first touched the man's ears and tongue. Then "He looked up to heaven," a plea to His heavenly Father for a miracle. Sighing deeply, He said, "Be opened" (Mark 7:31–35). Wonder overwhelmed the people as the man's ears were opened, his tongue was loosened, and he began to speak plainly.

When the disciples were unable to heal *a violently possessed boy*, Jesus ordered the demon to come out of the boy. Though no mention is made of any prayer by Jesus, He must have prayed because, later, when the disciples asked privately, "Why couldn't we drive it out?" He replied, "This kind can come out only by prayer" (Mark 9:14–29). Some manuscripts add, "and fasting," but the earlier ones have only "prayer." Though Jesus fasted and spoke of fasting to His followers, no mention is ever made of His fasting in connection with the times He prayed.

One day, moved by the sight of *a blind beggar*, Jesus spat on the ground, made mud, put it on the man's eyes, and told him to go wash in the pool of Siloam. The blind man obeyed. Suddenly he could see! His amazed neighbors brought the man to the Pharisees who conducted interrogations with both the man and his parents. Despite repeated firsthand testimony to the healing, the Pharisees would not admit that Jesus performed a miracle. Impatient with their failure to accept the miracle, the healed man turned the tables on them. "Now that is remarkable! You don't know where he comes from, yet he opened my eyes. We know that God does not listen to sinners. He listens to the godly man who does his will. Nobody has ever heard of opening the eyes of a man born blind. If this man were not from God, he could do nothing." At this point the Pharisees insulted and excommunicated the healed man (John 9:30–34).

Though no mention is made of Jesus praying in connection with this miracle, it is strongly implied in the words of the healed man when he said that God doesn't listen to sinners, but to godly men. Could it be that the blind man argued this way because he had heard Jesus ask God audibly to restore his sight?

The record states clearly that Jesus prayed before He performed His most dramatic miracle, *the raising of Lazarus* from the dead. Standing at the grave, Jesus ordered the stone removed from the entrance. Then He "looked up and said 'Father, I thank you that you have heard me. I knew that you always hear me'" (John 11:41–42). Then with loud voice Jesus called Lazarus forth.

Though Jesus was in a league all by Himself in performing miracles, and though He doesn't call us today to walk on water, He still performs mighty marvels in our behalf.

Several decades ago a German peasant, living near Warsaw, had been unable to pay his rent. When the landlord threatened to evict him, he begged for more time. The landlord replied that tomorrow he and his family would be turned out into the snow.

When the church bells chimed at evening prayer, the man knelt with his family, asking the Lord to supply their needs. Just then they heard a strange noise at the window. Opening it, they found a raven that his grandfather had tamed years before. In its beak was a valuable ring that had been lost that day by the king who was visiting the town. The man returned it, and the king gave him a reward of enough money to build his own house.

God doesn't always answer in such dramatic fashion. But He is still a God of wonder who responds to our prayers in crises.

When Abandoned on the Cross

As the culminating crisis approached—the hour of the Cross— Jesus prayed much. Luke records that during that last hectic week, "Each day Jesus was teaching at the temple, and each evening he went out to spend the night on the hill called the Mount of Olives" (Luke 21:37). The Gethsemane area was His customary place to pray. On Thursday evening, after observing the Passover and instituting the Lord's Supper, He went there to pray. His calm majesty in Pilate's judgment hall and the victory of Calvary were won those nights in the garden. Then came the crucifixion, and the fourth cry from the cross, the only cry recorded in more than one Gospel, "My God, my God, why have you forsaken me?" (Matt. 27:46; Mark 15:34).

In this emotional outburst Jesus was not only quoting, but fulfilling a statement uttered prophetically by David. The time was around 3 p.m. (Matt. 27:45). Jesus had been hanging on the cross for six hours, the last three shrouded in darkness. He had been ridiculed by the crowds, the soldiers, and at first by both thieves. By now the mockery had long subsided. The strange silence was punctuated by the heavy breathing and groaning of the victims. Then suddenly came the loud cry.

Who can fully understand it? It is reported that Martin Luther determined to study this cry of Jesus, and continued without food and in one position in his chair in his attempt to comprehend it. At length he rose and exclaimed, "God forsaken of God! Who can understand that?" We note that Jesus did not curse God, but dared to question Him, a consolation to those who at some time feel abandoned by God.

It is significant that this is the only time among the quoted prayers of Jesus that He did not address God as Father. On many occasions when Jesus prayed His words are not recorded. But when His prayers are directly quoted in the Gospels, every time, without fail, Jesus calls God "Father"—except here where He cries out, "My God, my God."

Why this exception? Somehow concentrated in those hours of suffering on the cross was all the divine punishment for human sin. Jesus was suffering the equivalent of hell in the stead of sinners. In some inexplicable manner the Father had turned from Him in the awful blackness, so that Jesus, feeling the separation, called out to Him as God, instead of as Father. It has been said that, to understand this cry, a person would need to go to hell, and go as the holy Son of God.

An Indian boy, as part of his initiation test, had to spend a night alone in the forest. His father led his son into the forest, collected wood, started a fire with instructions to keep it going all night, and promised to return first thing in the morning. All night the boy sweated and shivered in sheer terror. Every snapping twig convinced him a wild animal was stalking him. Finally, the seemingly interminable blackness of night gave way to the gray of dawn, enabling him to distinguish the trunks of the trees. As the light became brighter, he became aware that the tall shape that he imagined to be a tree trunk was a man standing motionless beside a tree. It was his father, and he had been there all the night.

Just as the Father had met Jesus' every crisis thus far, so now in the Son's final hour He did not desert Him, but was with Him all the time. Moments later Jesus cried, "It is finished," and then, "Father, into Thy hands I commit My spirit."

A king hired several people to make some tapestries for him with instructions to seek his advice immediately when any problem arose. Among the helpers was a boy who made steady progress while the others were troubled with many failures. One day they gathered around the youngster and asked, "Why are you successful while we're always making a mess? Either our material gets tangled up or turns out different from the pattern."

The boy answered, "Don't you remember the word of the king to send for him promptly if we needed help? You waited till things were snarled so badly that it took days to unravel them. Did you notice how often I called for him?"

"Yes," said the others, "but we thought he was very busy and didn't want to disturb him too often."

"Well," replied the boy, "I just took him at his word, and he was always happy to help me!"

Jesus, who called for the help of His Father when facing crisis, bids us to come to the throne of grace in time of need.

Notes
1. Pat Williams and Jill Williams with Jerry Jenkins, *Rekindled* (Grand Rapids: Revell, 1985).
2. F. L. Godet, *Commentary on the Gospel of Luke*, vol. 1 (Grand Rapids: Zondervan, n.d.), p. 412.

CHAPTER 6

Transforming Yourself

Corrie ten Boom and her sister, Betsy, were imprisoned in Ravensbruck concentration camp during World War II. In *The Hiding Place* Corrie relates many episodes of Betsy's Christlike behavior through months of misery. Many consider Betsy to be as notable a heroine as Corrie. But Betsy ultimately became ill, pale, and emaciated, a prematurely aged woman. She was taken to the prison hospital to die. Getting the news, Corrie was distraught. Amazingly, one of the nurses called Corrie to the mortuary to look upon the beautiful, fleshed-out body of her sister, her hair restored to its normal color, and the wrinkles of her face smoothed into an expression of deep peace. Corrie commented, "Perhaps this was exceptional, but Betsy was transformed in death."[1]

One of the extraordinary events in the life of Jesus was His transfiguration. About a week after Jesus began foretelling His death, He "took Peter, John and James with him and went up onto a mountain to pray. As he was praying, the appearance of his face changed, and his clothes became as bright as a flash of lightning" (Luke 9:28–29). Matthew says that "His face shone like the sun, and his clothes became as white as light" (17:2). Mark says that "His clothes became dazzling white, whiter than anyone in the world could bleach them" (9:3). The writers seemed to have difficulty describing His spectacularly luminous appearance.

The Transfiguration happened when Jesus was praying. Luke plainly says that Jesus went up into a mountain to pray. Matthew and Mark give the impression that He went into the mountain to let three of His disciples see Him transfigured. He had both purposes in mind. His glorification came as an answer to His praying. He prayed specifically for the revelation of His glory to these three disciples. Godet in his *Commentary on the Gospel of Luke,*[2] writing of the connection between the prayer of Jesus and His transfiguration, says that the preposition Luke uses "denotes more than a mere simultaneousness (while He prayed), and makes His prayer the cause of this mysterious event."

The object of the Transfiguration was to strengthen the faith of Peter, James, and John. This event occurred about a week after Jesus had shocked them with the announcement of His coming sufferings and violent death (Matt. 17:1; Mark 9:3; Luke 9:8). He had been repeating this same message in villages around Ceasarea Philippi. Each time they heard this dismal prophecy, they recoiled with abhorrence. How could the Messiah be treated so badly? They were bewildered, anxious, perhaps depressed. Whenever they gazed into the face of Jesus He looked just like other men. Was He really the Son of God? And how could the Son of God die? They needed a faith-lift job.

So to rouse them out of their week-long stupor of gloom, He prayed to His Father to strengthen these men by revealing His true nature and mission. If they could see, even if but for a few moments, that He was the Christ, the Son of the living God, this would cushion the announcement of His demise. He may have prayed something like this, "Grant these men a glimpse of the glory which I enjoyed with you in eternity past. Give them a view of the transfigured Messiah. Impress on their minds in vivid form who I really am. May the truth of this revelation never be forgotten. Help them to see the importance of My death—that to execute My Messianic mission I must be put to death—that the crown comes only after the Cross. Help them to see the splendor of the coming kingdom, and take up their cross and follow Me." Jesus in His thoughtful love would take the sting out of the bad news, confirm their faith, and prepare them for the ordeal of His passion.

Jesus Was Transfigured Before Them

While Jesus was praying on the mountain, probably one of the Hermon ranges, Peter, James, and John fell asleep. It was on awakening that they saw Jesus transfigured. His face was shining, not with reflected light as did that of Moses coming down from Sinai, but from a brilliance which burst forth from within and irradiated His clothes with a dazzling effulgence. Jesus' real nature was now showing through. In His heavenly, preincarnate days this glory had been part of His usual appearance. As a member of the Trinity, He had constantly shone with splendor. But on coming to earth, He hid this brilliance for thirty-three years, a remarkable feat. Why did He do so? It was part of His humiliation. At the incarnation He surrendered the outward dazzle of His deity. He was still God, but without His beaming radiance. He could have walked around Galilee and Judea with His glory shining forth in glittering majesty, but He humbly relinquished His glorious appearance during those years on earth. But at His transfiguration He resumed His outward glory for a few, fleeting moments of time.

The word for transfiguration also means metamorphosis, a scientific word referring to a change into one's real nature, like the turning of a caterpillar into a butterfly. Another Greek word, "transform," has the opposite meaning—the assuming of an outward expression not indicative of one's inward nature, as when Satan and false apostles masquerade as angels of light when inwardly full of darkness. Jesus' transfiguration was no masquerade. He did not put on an exterior that contradicted His inner nature. His real, inner nature was full of glory. For a few minutes, His intrinsic radiance broke through the veil of His humanity, revealing the glory which He had with the Father before the world began (John 17:5). Then, shortly after, He again surrendered His outer glory and assumed His normal human appearance the rest of His earthly days.

Jesus was a monarch who walked around wearing the disguise of rags, while hiding the robes of royalty beneath, His grandeur voluntarily eclipsed. Then for a brief period God turned Jesus inside out to show His true nature. (What if God turned us inside out and exposed our real inner life?)

The Transfiguration made an indelible impression on Peter,

James, and John. Jesus had told them that they would not taste death till they had seen the Son of Man coming in His kingdom (Luke 9:27). So on the mountainside He granted them a glimpse of His coming glory. The Transfiguration was a dress rehearsal of the kingdom and power which He would display at His Second Coming. Transfigured, He indeed looked like the Son of God.

Jesus Conversed with Moses and Elijah About His Coming Death

When Peter, James, and John awoke, shook off the fogginess of their senses, and became accustomed to the brightness, they not only saw Jesus in all His majesty, but also the forms of two men in glorious splendor who turned out to be Moses and Elijah. The three were engaged in a celestial conversation which must have held the disciples spellbound. Their dialogue dealt with Jesus' imminent death in Jerusalem. The word "departure" in Luke 9:31 is used by Peter to refer to his own death in 2 Peter 1:15. This centerpiece of conversation would convince the three disciples of the importance of His death. They had shrunk from the concept of His death, and now to their amazement learned that this theme was a priority item on the agenda of heaven. At the moment of Jesus' greatest display of glory, the two men who represented the Old Testament, Moses the law and Elijah the prophets, were talking about a subject which Peter had considered a shameful impossibility. Now Peter knows how wrong he was to have opposed Jesus' intent to die, that deity and death were not incompatible, that the Cross was no disgrace, that heaven was talking about it and waiting for it.

Impetuous Peter suggested building shelters for Jesus, Moses, and Elijah, so that the visit of these dignitaries could be prolonged. But a bright cloud enveloped them, from which a voice said, "This is my Son, whom I love; with him I am well pleased." The terrified apostles fell prostrate. Jesus touched them, reassuringly. Looking up, they saw no one but Jesus. Old Testament characters as illustrious as Moses and Elijah fade in the presence of Christ, leaving Him unchallenged, unique, and supreme. The Father's voice with its confirmation of approval must have been an encouragement to Jesus who must have thought often on the agony of the Cross. He would be strengthened in His resolve, and set His face toward Jerusalem. We note again that each of the three times the Father's voice speaks from heaven it came after Jesus prayed.

Jesus' prayer was answered. He desired to confirm the faith of these three apostles who would play so important a part in the founding of the church. They had been told of His death, but now had seen a foretaste of His coming glory. The memory of that scene would carry them through Gethsemame and Golgotha, even though they would temporarily falter. The Transfiguration would help James face martyrdom by the sword. It would help Peter sleep the night before his scheduled but thwarted execution, knowing that reunion with Jesus awaited him. John and Peter both wrote of the Transfiguration. John said simply, "We have seen His glory, the glory of the One and Only" (John 1:14). Peter wrote, "We did not follow cleverly invented stories when we told you about the power and coming of our Lord Jesus Christ, but we were eyewitnesses of his majesty. For he received honor and glory from God the Father when the voice came to him from the Majestic Glory, saying, 'This is my Son, whom I love; with him I am well pleased.' We ourselves heard this voice that came from heaven when we were with him on the sacred mountain (2 Peter 1:16–18).

The Impact of our Praying on Ourselves

Some regard prayer as a form of psychological therapy in which we merely converse with ourselves in a sort of inner pep talk that helps us over the rough spots of life. To some, prayer has subjective value only.

But others rightly emphasize the objective value of prayer. God does hear and answer us. Prayer produced definite results in Jesus' ministry. His praying affected people and events, and was never simply an exercise in psychotherapy.

The solution to the problem is not an either-or. Prayer has both objective and subjective values. Its primary purpose is to move God to act. The prayers of Jesus resulted in objective results. But prayer has a secondary, but genuine, psychological value. The one who prays may benefit subjectively from communing with God. The act of praying does do something to the one praying. Jesus was praying when He was transfigured. Through prayer believers can experience transformed lives. Charles R. Erdman says, "When in prayer his followers find, in some measure, what it is to be transfigured into his likeness from one degree of glory to another by the power of his indwelling Spirit."[3]

Some of the subjective benefits of prayer may be physical. In an address to the British Medical Association, a prominent physician said, "The best medicine I've discovered is prayer. I would state that of all hygienic measures to counteract disturbed sleep, depression of spirit, and a distressed mind, I would undoubtedly give first place to the simple habit of prayer. It does more to quiet the spirit and strengthen the soul than any other therapeutic agency known to man."[4]

Dr. Alexis Carrell, Nobel Prize winner in medicine, said, "The influence of prayer on the human mind and body is as demonstrable as that of the secreting glands. . . . As a physician I have seen men, after all other therapy had failed, lifted out of disease and melancholy by the serene effort of prayer."[5]

Light comes at the beginning of the Christian life

It's a simple prayer that brings the first glimmer of light into the heart. Jesus told of two men who went up to the temple to pray. The proud Pharisee's prayer was essentially a series of boasts, "I," "I," "I." The sinful tax-collector would not lift his eyes (nor his "I's") to heaven, but smote upon his breast, begging, "God, have mercy on me, a sinner." Jesus said the tax collector went home justified in the sight of God. When the consciousness of sins forgiven dawned on that publican, he would have been filled with a joy soon reflected in his face.

In the *Walker Family Saga,* Robert Walker traces his family history through the eleven generations from the Plymouth, Massachusetts, landing in 1635. Near the end he tells of the prayer that first brought the light to his own heart around 1930. Enrolling in Wheaton College to play football, he found himself totally incompatible with the strong Christian environment. Well-meaning fellow students stuffed his mailbox with religious tracts, as well as shoving them under the door of his dormitory room. Antagonized, he decided to change colleges.

Late that summer his parents suggested a trip to Michigan's Upper Peninsula to escape his usual hay fever. When the weather turned bad for fishing, Bob read everything he had brought along. Picking up an old Bible at the camp one day, he asked, "Ugh, who can understand it?" Then he wondered, "But there must be a creator somewhere. The people at Wheaton College said it was the God of the Bible." Thoughtfully he turned the pages, "If You are the God who inspired this book," he said to himself, "You should be able to reveal Yourself to me. A preacher or evangelist shouldn't be necessary. And if You do, I will follow You."

He said, "Probably my prayer was shorter than that, but as I look back now, it seems to me this was my moment of truth. For God clearly answered my prayer. During the next ten days I spent 6–8 hours a day reading and gradually comprehending the Book that once had been closed to me. When I left camp, I knew I was a changed person." [6]

When Bob walked onto the campus at Northwestern that fall, for the first time in his life he knew what his profession was to be—journalism, hopefully involving Christian writing and editing. And it did. Bob Walker became a pioneer in Christian journalism. He founded and edited InterVarsity's *His* magazine, as well as *Christian Life* magazine, taught journalism at Wheaton College, started Christian Writers Institute correspondence school and Creation House Publishers, besides inspiring many into Christian writing, including both my wife and me.

Through a prayer, Bob's life had been illumined by the Light of the world who had shone in his heart to give him the knowledge of the glory of God in the face of Christ (2 Cor. 4:6). And he had the subjective joy that comes through a new relationship to Jesus Christ. Illumination does not come to all in the same way, but when it comes, it brings an inner glow.

Continuing transformation gives strength and poise

Prayer not only brings initial enlightenment but continues to provide power and poise in times of need. Hubert and Bettie Addleton, missionaries in hot, dusty, interior Pakistan, saw very little fruit during their first term. Returning for their second term, Hubert became very discouraged, especially after bouts of malaria and hepatitis. When he traveled by train 200 miles to a hospital in Karachi, his wife, knowing the state of his mind and body, packed their possessions to return to the USA.

As he lay on his hospital bed, he studied Ephesians, asking that Paul's prayer for that "incomparable great power" available for believers (1:18–19) might be displayed in his own life. He prayed, "Lord, give me the strength to keep on serving You here for another year and show me something of Your power this year."

He and his wife went back to their mission station and continued their witness for Christ. One day a man knocked at their courtyard door. He had picked up a leaflet they had tossed to him on the road near his village, which advertised their Bible correspondence course. He had written for the course, and through it had become a believer. He wanted the Addletons to come and baptize him and his immediate family whom he had led to Christ. Because of extreme busyness on the mission station, the Addletons delayed in fulfilling his request.

Soon after, one morning at 5 a.m., Addleton answered the door in his pajamas. This same man had come the 80 miles to the missionary's house with six members of his family. He said that since the missionary hadn't come to them, they were coming to the missionaries for teaching and baptism! The Addletons found a place for them for a few days, taught them the basics of the Gospel, and baptized them in a nearby irrigation canal. The convert became a very effective evangelist, leading thousands of his Hindu tribal people to faith in Jesus.

Says Addleton, "The Lord heard my cry from the hospital bed and gave me this sign that He wanted us to stay in Pakistan." Strengthened by this answer to prayer, they are still serving there at this writing in 1993.

John Henry Strong, son of the theologian, Augustus H. Strong, says, "From a purely natural point of view, I suppose that I should never have been a clergyman. Serious illness in my boyhood had left me with ravaged nerves, so that as I grew up, I saw every task as though I were marching to the slaughter. Often, lying exhausted on my bed after a morning service and unable even to contemplate a service for the evening of that day, I have begun to run through the promises of God to repair the vanished strength of those who seek him: 'They that wait upon the LORD shall renew their strength; they shall mount up with wings as eagles; they shall run, and not be weary; and they shall walk, and not faint' (Isa. 40:31 KJV). 'My grace is sufficient for thee: for my strength is made perfect in weakness' (2 Cor. 12:9 KJV). 'Wait on the Lord: . . . and he shall strengthen thine heart' (Ps. 27:14 KJV). Repeating these and similar words, I have soon found myself saying, 'I can do all things in Him that strengtheneth me.' My weariness had vanished. The thing promised had passed into me. I have stood up, met my appointments, and ended the day with wonder, thanksgiving and praise."[7]

Henry Stanley, famous journalist who found Livingstone in the heart of Africa, wrote, "On all my expeditions, prayer made me stronger, morally and mentally, than any of my nonpraying companions. It did not blind my eyes, or dull my mind, or close my ears; but on the contrary, it gave me confidence. It did more; it gave me joy and pride in my work, eager to face the day's perils.'"[8]

Jesus said that we ought always to pray, and not to faint. Praying gives us courage and cool in the midst of turmoil.

Our transformation is a continuing process

Paul wrote, "And we, who with unveiled faces all reflect the Lord's glory, are being transformed into his likeness with ever-increasing glory" (2 Cor. 3:18). Paul spoke from experience. In his early years he had a veil over his eyes, which not only kept him from seeing the glory of Jesus, but also led him to persecute Jesus' followers. Then one day on the Damascus Road a blazing light, brighter than the noonday sun, shone on him and removed the veil. From the moment of his enlightenment, Paul poured out his life in carrying the light to the ends of the world. As the years went by, His desire was to become more like Jesus and to reflect His glory to others.

After our initial looking to Jesus for salvation, we continue beholding Him. We set our affection on things above, because earthly idols can so easily blur our focus. We see Him in the Scripture, the living Word in the written Word. We note His divine excellencies where "majestic sweetness sits enthroned upon the Savior's brow." We turn our eyes upon Jesus, gaze full in His wonderful face, so that the things of earth grow strangely dim in the light of His glory and grace. Thereby we fulfill Paul's command, "Do not conform any longer to the pattern of this world, but be transformed by the renewing of your mind" (Rom. 12:2). The right attitude of mind, prompted by scriptural truth and prayer, helps us overcome an improper outlook and a wrong lifestyle. Prayer promotes our spiritual transformation. Incidentally, the word for "transformed" in Romans 12:2 is the same word used of Jesus' transfiguration.

Prayer changes things and prayer changes us. It is said that we become like those we live with. After years of marriage, husbands and wives often take on the habits of their mates. It is possible to so keep company with Jesus as to fall into His habits, learn to walk like Him, talk like Him, think as He thinks, and love as He loves. Richard J. Foster says the purpose of prayer "is to bring us into such a life of communion with the Father that, by the power of the Spirit, we are increasingly conformed to the image of the Son."[9]

Transformation is a progressive process, continuing until that day when we are presented faultless before God's throne.

A godly glow

Though no mortal will ever shine with the brilliance of Jesus, some believers seem to reflect a small measure of divine radiance. *The Pulpit Commentary* on the Transfiguration in Luke 9:29 says, "Real, close communion with God ever imparts to the countenance of the one who has thus entered into communion with the High and Holy One, a new and strange beauty. Very many have noticed at times the peculiar and lovely change pass over the faces of God's true saints as they prayed—faces perhaps old and withered, gray with years and wrinkled with care."[10]

Moses' face shone after he had communed with God on the mount. As Stephen pleaded his case before the council in Jerusalem, the members of the Sanhedrin looked intently at him, "and they saw that his face was like the face of an angel" (Acts 6:15). Though not all saints reflect the brightness of God physically in their face, some saints who spend time in the quiet place seem to radiate an aura of the celestial Presence.

One man who mirrored the heavenly glow was Robert Murray McCheyne, Scottish pastor, evangelist, and man of prayer, who died in his thirtieth year. One contemporary said, "McCheyne's holiness was noticeable even before he spoke a word; his appearance spoke for him." Another wrote, "Often has the remark been made that he was the most faultless and attractive exhibition of the true Christian which they had ever seen embodied in a living form. His great study was to be Christlike. Hence, he carried with him a kind of hallowing influence into every company into which he entered." A letter, addressed to him by an unknown hearer who had heard his last discourse, and found unopened on his desk after his death, contained these words, "It was not so much what you said, as your manner of speaking, that struck me. I saw in you a holiness that I never saw before."

After speaking of the possibility of having a radiant countenance, the Quaker scholar Rufus Jones was approached by a woman "with an almost unbelievably plain face" who asked him what he would do if he had a face like hers. He replied, "While I have troubles of my own of that kind, I've discovered that if you light up from within, any old face you have is good enough."[11]

Brother Lawrence is known for his practice of the presence of God. Because of his habit of constant prayer, others said of him that the very expression of his face with its calm appearance was edifying; that he was never hasty or loitering, but did each thing at its proper time with an even, uninterrupted composure of spirit; that in the noise and clatter when several persons were calling for different things at the same time he possessed a God-given tranquillity as if on his knees.

Prayer is a source of joy and contentment which often shows on the face of the believer. Before he became a missionary to Burma, Adoniram Judson wrote in his diary, "I have this day attained more than ever to what I suppose Christians mean by the enjoyment of God. I have had pleasant seasons at the throne of God." The psalmist testified, "In thy presence is fulness of joy; at thy right hand are pleasures for evermore" (16:11 KJV). Jesus said, "Ask and you will receive, and your joy will be complete" (John 16:24).

Beautiful faces are those that seem
With the very love of God to beam;
Beautiful forms are those that grace
With gentle service the lowliest place.

—Anonymous

The Influence of Your Praying On Others

When Jesus took little children in His arms, His prayer blessing not only invoked the welfare of the children but also, since the children were too young to comprehend, carried psychological benefits to the parents. Parents would be reminded of God's goodness in blessing their homes with those, precious, little bundles of life, as well as their responsibility to rear them in the training and instruction of the Lord.

When Jesus prayed before raising Lazarus, it was partly for the benefit of the bystanders to show that the ensuing miracle was performed by God's power in direct answer to Jesus' prayer.

When Jesus prayed privately, but within sight of the disciples, He created in them an intense desire to learn to pray. Simply hearing another praying may have a psychological effect on the observer. Could it be that James, the brother of Jesus who became known for his devout prayer habits, though not converted till after the Resurrection, imbibed his devotion to prayer from quietly observing Jesus during their family years together in Nazareth before Jesus left home? One lady attests to the profound impact, when a little girl, of finding her father praying. It did more good than several Sunday school lessons.

Persecutor Saul could never forget Stephen's shining face—it became a goad that helped drive him into the arms of Jesus.

Philip Yancey in *Christianity Today* tells of a visit to large prison in Chile where he attended a service with a congregation of 150 prisoners. On the platform a band of eighteen guitarists, one accordionist, and two men wielding handmade brass tambourines led a rousing song service. The inmates wore a variety of handed-down street clothes. The service went on gathering enthusiasm. Prisoners took turns giving testimonies, and many spontaneously knelt at rough wooden benches to pray.

Later Yancey, along with the chaplain and the other visiting

Prison Fellowship workers, were invited to meet with the prison psychologist, sociologist, and social workers. The prison staff professionals discussed the effect of the Christian faith on the prisoners. They seemed to view it with mild tolerance—a little dose of religion couldn't hurt. However, the chaplain and Prison Fellowship workers contended that their work contributed far more. Using statistics, they held that rehabilitation failed unless it included the prisoners' spiritual needs.

After thirty minutes of discussion, the warden reached his toleration limit. Sitting there with his bushy mustache, sallow face, huge barrel chest covered with rows of military ribbons, he spoke up, and everyone fell silent. "It doesn't matter to me which faith these prisoners take to," he declared with finality. "But it's clear they need to change, and they'll never do it without some outside assistance." As he spoke, the singing of prisoners in the courtyard could still be heard. "Chaplain," he continued, "one-third of the men in this facility attend your services. You visit several times a week, but I'm here every day. And I tell you, those men are different. They don't just put on a performance when you come around—they are different than the other prisoners. They have a joy. They share with other prisoners. They care about more than themselves. And so I think we ought to do all we can to help this fine work." The warden's statement immediately ended the discussion. Prayer had changed inmate deportment and indelibly impressed the warden.

Transformed, we reflect Him to others. A wealthy family invited a Christian leader to be a guest in their home for a week. The maid, shopping, sneered, "Some saint is coming to speak, and my master is entertaining him. I must have the finest cut of meat. You'd think the Lord Himself was coming." A few days later a subdued maid returned for more meat. The butcher asked how things were going with the saintly visitor. Meekly she replied, "A few days ago I said you'd think the Lord was coming. I want you to know I think I have seen the Lord this week." [12]

Your praying can transform you and influence others.

Notes
1. Corrie ten Boom, *The Hiding Place* (Old Tappan, N.J.: Fleming H. Revell, 1971).

2. F. L. Godet, *Commentary on the Gospel of Luke* vol. 1 (Grand Rapids: Zondervan, n.d.), p. 45.
3. Charles R. Eerdman, *The Gospel of Luke* (Philadelphia: Westminster Press, 1949), p. 98.
4. *Our Daily Bread,* 19 August 1991.
5. Alexis Carrell, *Robins Reader* (Richmond, Va.: A. H. Robins Co., Inc., January, 1954).
6. Robert Walker, *Walker Family Saga,* pp. 65–67.
7. John Henry Strong, *Jesus, The Man of Prayer* (Judson Press, 1945), pp. 49–50.
8. *Our Daily Bread,* 15 September 1993.
9. Richard J. Foster, *Prayer: Finding the Heart's True Home* (San Francisco: HarperCollins, 1992), p. 57.
10. *The Pulpit Commentary* (Funk and Wagnalls, n.d.)
11. *Our Daily Bread,* 7 December 1992.
12. Philip Yancey, *Christianity Today,* 5 February 1988.

CHAPTER 7

Teaching the Disciples to Pray

Armin Gesswein, prayer chairman for many Billy Graham crusades, had an experience early in his ministry which completely changed his understanding of prayer. One night an elderly man walked into a weekly prayer meeting Gesswein had just started. He continued coming each week. Whenever he prayed Gesswein detected something new. "I have never heard praying like that," he said to himself. It was not just fervency—Gesswein had plenty of that. His praying had a strange immediacy about it. Heaven and earth got together when the man prayed. Prayer and answer were not far apart. "But," said Gesswein, "when I prayed, God was way out in the distance, and the answer, too, seemed in the distant bye and bye." Eager to learn his secret, Gesswein went to see Uncle Am, a retired blacksmith and Methodist lay preacher.

Gesswein said, "Uncle Am, I would love to pray with you." At once the elderly man arose, led Gesswein outside across the driveway into a red barn, up a ladder, and into a haymow. There in some old hay lay two big Bibles, one open. Wondering about the Bibles, Gesswein prayed first, pouring out his heart to God. Then Uncle Am prayed, and again "that difference." There in the hay, on their knees, at eyeball level, Gesswein said, "Uncle Am, what is it? You have some kind of a secret in praying. Would you mind sharing it with me?"

Gesswein was twenty-four; Uncle Am was seventy-three. With an eagle look he said, "Young man, learn to plead the promises of God." He meant that we should fill our hearts with Bible promises, and when a need arises, find the promise that fits that need, claim it, and God will delight in fulfilling His own Word. Gesswein said, "That did it! My praying was never the same thereafter."

The Disciples' Request

One day after the last Feast of Tabernacles, only months away from the Cross, when Jesus had finished praying, one of His disciples said, "Lord, teach us to pray, just as John taught his disciples" (Luke 11:1). Although we don't know which disciple made the request, it's likely he voiced what all the others were desiring in their hearts. It wasn't as if the disciples were strangers to prayer. Devout Jews of their time were conversant with the rich heritage of Jewish prayers and blessings. They had their houses of prayer, their psalms of prayer, their morning, afternoon, and evening prayers, their special benedictions before and after meals, all ingrained in the culture of the day. But Jesus' prayer habits were so different from those of the Pharisees. Never had a man prayed as Jesus prayed. And they wished to learn how. What factors led to their request?

The disciples had noted Jesus' faithful prayer habits. They had been in His constant company for over two years, and He was still adhering to His policy of regular private praying. Wherever He went on His travels, He customarily found a private spot and went aside to pray alone. This time it was no different. Here He was again "in a certain place," praying, consistent in His prayer practice.

Some contend, "Prayer is a state of mind. I never pray at a specific time or place. I pray without ceasing. I'm always in the attitude of prayer." Jesus was always in the attitude of prayer but to Him prayer was also more than a mood; prayer involved a definite place and time. Our text says, "One day Jesus was praying in a certain place," and "When he finished. . . ."

The disciples were impressed from first-hand observation of Jesus' praying. An elderly man in West Africa spent several weeks at a dispensary recovering from illness. One day on a missionary's porch he said he wanted to become a believer. The missionary quizzed him to test the reality of his faith. His testimony showed depth of understanding. Asked who had helped him come to this decision, he answered, "Tyekpele." Tyekpele was an older woman who helped with the cleaning, lived at the dispensary, and had a strong influence among the patients in the transient quarters. The elderly man said, "When Tyekpele prays, I pick up my ears and listen."

How often the disciples had seen Jesus at prayer. Often when Jesus prayed in a solitary place, His disciples were present, able to see Him and close enough to converse with Him as at the Transfiguration, in Gethsemane, and in Luke 9:18. Does not His praying in front of His disciples seem inconsistent with His warning against praying in public, "When you pray, do not be like the hypocrites, for they love to pray standing in the synagogues and on the street corners to be seen by men. . . . When you pray, go into your room, close the door and pray to your Father" (Matt. 6:5–6). How do we reconcile this apparent inconsistency?

Jesus never condemned praying in public per se. In fact, He prayed publicly at the feeding of the five thousand. He blessed little children in a crowd of parents. He prayed in the midst of a grieving group before raising Lazarus. What He forbade was not public prayer, but ostentatious praying.

At a ministerial conference a preacher, called on to pray, uttered a flowery supplication that someone called "the million dollar prayer." Admittedly, a person who prays in a service must remember that he represents an entire congregation, and may find that pondering his prayer in advance makes for better worship. But this is no license to tickle ears by the delivery of a pompous composition, like the seminary student who used to open a window and pray at the top of his lungs.

The Greek verb, "to be seen," gives us our English "theater." Jesus denounced praying to the grandstand, scorching the teachers who devoured widows' houses and "for a show made lengthy prayers" (Mark 12:40). Jesus never offered a prayer for the disciples to admire, but did allow them to see Him pray, hoping to stir in them a fascination for praying. They soon became painfully aware of their deficiency.

Did the disciples do more than see Jesus praying? Could they hear what He said? When He prayed in public His words were there for all to hear. For example, He prayed at the feeding of the five thousand, at the blessing of little children, at the visit of the Greeks, and at the grave of Lazarus. But what about His private praying near the disciples? Did He pray silently? If aloud, could they make out the words? If at the Transfiguration Jesus was close enough for the disciples to overhear His conversation with Moses and Elijah, could we not conclude that Jesus was close enough for them to overhear the words of His praying before they fell asleep?

In Gethsemane Jesus prayed a "stone's throw" away from the disciples (Luke 22:41). Whether it's possible to hear from that distance depends on the size of the stone, the strength of the thrower, the volume of the voice, and the sharpness of the ear. People are usually able to hear a speaker a stone's throw away, even without amplification. Hebrews 5:17 is thought to refer to Jesus' praying in Gethsemane, "During the days of Jesus' life on earth, he offered up prayers and petitions with loud cries and tears to the one who could save him from death. . . ." Whenever Jesus prayed aloud, would He not articulate loudly and clearly, even though not under the same strain as in the Garden?

G. Campbell Morgan says that the request to be taught to pray came "when His disciples had watched; and I think possibly had listened to Him praying alone. They had seen Him, and they had possibly heard Him; and His praying inspired them with a passion to do the same thing"[1]

The Disciples Considered Prayer the Key to Jesus' Success

After two years of close association the disciples concluded that prayer was the reason for the power in His ministry. Much as they were struck with His teachings, they were more impressed with the results of His praying. His wondrous deeds in public resulted from His prayer in private. Over and over they had witnessed cloistered intercession, then had watched Him go out and perform marketplace marvels. He demonstrated that difficult demons could be cast out only by prayer (Mark 9:29). Clearly prayer was the means by which He accomplished things. Note that they didn't ask, "Teach us to communicate," or "Teach us to heal," or "Teach us to walk on water." Rather it was "Lord, teach us to pray."

The disciples wanted a concrete model to follow. One commentator emphasizes that the request didn't say, "Teach us how to pray," but simply, "Teach us to pray." Granted—there is a difference between *telling* and *teaching.* Telling gives a theoretical list of pointers, but teaching requires practical, hands-on coaching. No lady could call herself a piano teacher if all she did was verbally instruct a pupil about piano-playing without showing how to do it. A batting coach doesn't merely lecture on the fine points of hitting, but shows a batter how to hold the bat and models his instruction. So, the commentator notwithstanding, when the disciples asked Jesus to teach them to pray, they were really asking Him to teach them how. *Phillips' Modern English* translation renders the disciples' request, "Lord, teach us *how* to pray, as John used to teach his disciples." The NIV translates Jesus' preface to the Lord's Prayer in the Sermon on the Mount, "This, then, is *how* you should pray" (Matt. 6:9). *Teaching* and *teaching how* are virtually synonymous.

What the disciples meant was something like this, "We want more than a lecture on prayer. Give us an example. What should we ask for? What words should we use? How do we go about it? Coach us just as John the Baptist taught his disciples." It was customary for rabbis to give simple formulas for their students to use. John the Baptist apparently did so for his followers.

It all came together one day. Stirred by the sight of their Master praying, or by catching a special word or solemn expression here and there, or by the way He spoke as friend to friend, one of the disciples spoke out a request that had been simmering in all their minds. His praying had always intrigued them, but at this point the growing interest culminated in an explicit appeal for special assistance and direction.

Jesus' Answer

In response, Jesus gave a model prayer known as "The Lord's Prayer," a misnomer since Jesus could not have joined in asking, "Forgive us our sins." Many prefer to label it, "The Disciples' Prayer," since it is Jesus' primer on prayer for His followers. It has been called the "alphabet of all possible petitions," for it contains all the major elements of spiritual and physical needs summed with totality in a few, choice, concise requests, ranging from the coming of the kingdom to food. This prayer has been recited for centuries, sometimes sincerely, sometimes superficially, in cathedrals and in slums. The Church of the Pater Noster on the Mount of Olives has the Lord's Prayer printed on its walls in forty-seven languages.

Did Jesus intend this prayer as a formula to be slavishly and mechanically repeated? Although He did not forbid its verbatim use, He did denounce the thoughtless recital of ritual prayer. Prayers are meaningful only if they come from the heart. Interestingly, our English word "patter" comes from the first word in the Lord's Prayer, "Paternoster." "Pater" is Latin for "father." Patter, according to the dictionary, means to chatter glibly or quickly uttered, as in the rapid-fire speech of an auctioneer, or pitch of a salesman, and had its origin in the meaningless recitation of the Lord's prayer in earlier centuries.

Nothing Jesus says in connection with the prayer indicates He intended it to be regularly recited in worship services. Nor was it ever mentioned in the book of Acts or in any of the epistles.

Seminary Professor Howard Hendricks told of a new Christian attending his first prayer meeting and afraid to pray because he couldn't articulate as easily as the others. But after some encouragement he rose and said, "Lord, this is Jim. I'm the one that met You last Thursday night. Forgive me, Lord, because I can't say it the way the rest of these people do, but I want to tell You the best I know how: I love You, Amen." Hendricks said that man's simple prayer ignited the meeting.

If the Lord's Prayer is not mandated for verbatim recital, may we use it in our church liturgy or personal devotions? Of course we may, as long as we think of the words and don't simply repeat them mechanically. The employment of the pronouns "us" and "our" indicate the appropriateness of congregational usage. On the positive side, its usage may help us articulate the yearnings of our heart, free us from the task of choosing correct words and phrases, remove the temptation to be cute or clever, and broaden our horizons beyond our petty, selfish concerns. The prayer seems more suggestive than exhaustive, a model on which to expand our petitions, and a guide to the spirit and tenor with which to approach the throne.

The Lord's Prayer

In this remarkable listing of petitions (Luke 11:2–4) the first two point to God's affairs, and the last three summarize man's needs. The first segment expresses aspiration to see God's program fully accomplished on this earth: "Your name," "Your kingdom." The second segment turns to pressing human concerns; "our bread," "our sins," our "temptation." This prayer ranges from God to man, from heaven to earth, and legitimates a wide spectrum of physical and spiritual needs as objects for prayer. No human could compress the deep, varied, and many wants of the human race into so few words. The same hands that made the oceans, built the Andes, and hung the sun, gave this prayer.

Invocation—"Father"

Some New Testament manuscripts have, "Our Father in heaven." Imagine looking up and calling God our Father. No Old Testament saint addressed God as Father. One purpose in Jesus coming to earth was to reveal the Fatherhood of God. His death on the cross made it possible for sinners to become children of God. Although God is the Father of all mankind in the sense of Creator, not everyone can call God Father in an intimate family relationship. Only those who receive Jesus as Savior become sons and daughters of the heavenly Father, and have this right (John 1:12–13).

The word for Father is the Aramaic word used by a little child calling his earthly father, "Abba," the equivalent of "Daddy." Its source may be found in the prattling syllables of a little child, "dada," "mama," "abba." The word indicates trust, intimacy, access, and security in a heavenly Father who is easily approachable and deeply loving. Children depend on their daddies for food and clothing. Jesus taught that if earthly fathers gave gifts to their children, how much more would their heavenly Father give good things to those that ask (Matt. 7:11). Sadly, abused children may have trouble with the Fatherhood concept.

Our God is omnipotent. How futile to pray to a helpless god of wood or stone! "Our" shows solidarity with other believers.

Our God who is omnipresent makes His special abode in heaven.

We address ourselves to His exalted throne, infinitely above us. Thus intimacy is balanced with reverence. Haddon Robinson says, "I cannot imagine the men and women of the Bible talking about 'the big Man upstairs.' To say God is our Father does not imply that God is a great big huggable teddy bear. The Bible keeps the tension between intimacy and awe." Speaking of the throne of grace to which we are bidden to come boldly, he adds, "That fact that we come to a throne should fill us with awe. But because it is a throne of grace, it is approachable. The sovereign almighty God of the universe has allowed us, because of Jesus Christ, to approach Him in prayer and address Him as Father"[2]

Aspirations Godward

Petition 1

In Hebrew history parents did not choose a name for their child to please a rich aunt or because it sounded nice. Parents selected a name hoping that child would grow up to personify the character expressed by that name. Similarly, early Americans gave their daughters names like Charity, Hope, and Patience.

The name of God stands for the character of God. God's names reveal His perfections and attributes. To hallow His name equals, "Cause Your name to be hallowed," or "May God be set apart as Someone special." It is to ask that the One who bears that name be honored, not disgraced. To hallow God's name means departing from evil behavior. "Everyone who confesses the name of the Lord must turn away from wickedness" (2 Tim. 2:19).

Petition 2

The Bible promises a golden era when righteousness will prevail and suffering and sorrow will be no more. This kingdom will become a reality at the Second Coming of Jesus. We pray and look forward to the climax of history when the kingdoms of this world become the kingdoms of our God and of His Christ.

Although the full establishment of the kingdom is a future event, there is a sense in which the kingdom is now here. Jesus said, "the kingdom of God is within you" (Luke 17:21). When we now personally submit to the authority of King Jesus, we come under His rule and become part of His kingdom. When I pray for His kingdom to come, I am virtually saying that I will cast down every idol and enthrone Him as King of every aspect of my life, including my talents, money, and marriage.

This petition reminds us that we live in enemy territory. Since this world is no friend to God, many times we may have to stand against the evil of current culture. We will reach out and help extend His kingdom by bringing those whose lives we touch under submission to Him. This embraces praying for churches and missionaries as they carry out the Great Commission. Wheaton College's motto reads, "For Christ and His Kingdom."

At this point many New Testament manuscripts include a petition closely related to the kingdom prayer, "May Your will be done on earth as it is in heaven." When God's kingdom is fully here, His will shall be completely done on earth as in heaven where angels do His bidding cheerfully and immediately.

In the meanwhile we must seek His will in our individual lives. Too often we subconsciously pray, "Your will be done providing it doesn't conflict with mine." We want success, money, and promotion, forgetting what we wish may harm us. On the other hand, adversity may be a blessing in disguise to conform us to the image of His Son. "Thy will be done" is not an easy prayer to offer in the face of an actual situation that blocks our ambitions. In the garden Jesus shrank from the events of the next twenty-four hours, but He prayed, "Not my will, but Yours."

Not only passive submission, but active obedience is required: in business conduct, in family life, in social contacts, in church and political relationships. It means no cheating by employees, no oppression by employers, no improper role modeling by parents, no disobedience by children, no meanness to neighbors, no backbiting of churchmembers, no false charges nor underhanded deals in public office. This prayer requires our own high level of righteous conduct.

Needs Manward

Petition 3—"Give us each day our daily bread"

What a seeming comedown from the first two petitions! After dealing with aspirations for God's name and kingdom, the prayer turns downward to man's needs. And the first need is so basic, so earthy, and so simple—bread. From the heights of heaven to mundane food. But isn't an army general interested in food for his soldiers? Does not our Father in heaven concern Himself with bread for His children on earth?

God is concerned about small matters. He wants us to depend on Him for items as secular and temporal as groceries. During His three years with the disciples, Jesus did not feed them in any miraculous way except in the case of the five thousand and four thousand, and in both cases He ordered them to gather up the leftovers. Bread would not always be plentiful. At times the disciples gleaned unpicked fruit from trees already harvested.

Millions around the world do not have daily bread. I vividly recall looking down from a Chicago elevated train one morning to see a homeless man tipping over a garbage can, scooping out discarded food, and stuffing it in his mouth. How utterly dependent we are on God for our food. Before every harvest we are just a few dwindling supplies of grain away from starvation. We should be thankful for every meal. Bread stands for the related activities required to earn it: job, health, transportation, and clothes. The petition does not ask for a vanload, not even a week's supply. It asks for necessities, not luxuries; bread, not cake. And we are to share with the hungry.

Petition 4—"Forgive us our sins, for we also forgive everyone who sins against us."
As bread is the basic need of the body, so forgiveness is the first need of the soul. Because man is more than body, he cannot live by bread alone. A part of him, made in the image of God and marred by sin, can never know peace till it receives forgiveness. Comfort cannot be derived from material mercies when the conscience is burdened with guilt.

Because of our failure to obey God's laws, we stand guilty before His bar of justice. God's record book has a full listing of our every sin, omission, and commission. Call them whatever we choose, failure, shortcoming, complex, or genetic trait, they are still trespasses or moral debts, which, if unpaid, will mean eternal separation from God. But here's the gospel undergirding this petition. Jesus came to earth to die on the cross for our sins. He paid it all. Through His grace, His blood will forgive our sins, apart from any goodness of ours. After our entrance into the family of God through repentance and faith, we need to maintain fellowship with our heavenly Father by regularly asking forgiveness for sins committed in our daily living.

This petition links our asking for forgiveness with our forgiveness of others. If we have been forgiven, we must forgive others who sin against us, not so as to be forgiven by God, but because we have been forgiven by God. If we have experienced the forgiveness of God, the resultant spirit of joy should lead to forgiving others. If we fail to exhibit a spirit of forgiveness toward others, perhaps we should examine our hearts to see if we have genuinely experienced divine forgiveness. This was the gist of Jesus' only comment on the Lord's Prayer in Matthew (6:14–15). Forgiveness doesn't mean that we forget, or that we don't keep hurting, or that we pretend it never happened, but rather that we don't let the offense drive a wedge between us and the offender. Jesus practiced what He taught, even on the cross, where His first cry was a prayer for His enemies.

Petition 5—"And lead us not into temptation"

Some manuscripts add, "but deliver us from the evil one," a clause which gives much of the same idea.

The 1992 *World Almanac* said that travelers to Russia were now welcome to visit Chernobyl, the site of the 1986 nuclear accident that released deadly radiation to the surrounding area, and to tour the radioactive waste dump nearby, and the concrete sarcophagus built around the reactor. Visitors were promised a free radiation test at both the start and finish of the tour, and if needed, medical treatment at no extra charge. Most of us would think long and hard before accepting such an offer.[3]

After initial forgiveness we need protection from the traps set by our enemy. We should value our spiritual life too highly to expose ourselves to needless danger. This petition says, "Keep me from yielding to temptation. Watch over me and protect me so that the devil, the evil world system, and my sinful flesh do not deceive me into doctrinal error and disreputable deeds."

The Christian life is a perilous journey. Sometimes God permits us to be tested like Job. John Bunyan in *Pilgrim's Progress* speaks of a road with a ditch on one side and quagmire on the other, and along the way the Slough of Despond, By-Path Meadow, Doubting Castle, Mountain of Error, Broad Way Gate, Dead Man's Lane, and Vanity Fair. This petition realizes Satan's strength, admits our weakness, and pleads the greater power of God so that though tempted, we may win the final victory.

The doxology commonly recited at the end of the Lord's Prayer is not found in early manuscripts. "For Yours is the kingdom and the power and the glory forever" may have been added in public recitation much the same way we add "Amen" at the end of hymns. This addenda focuses attention on the glory of God. Praying the Lord's Prayer helps keep us from publicizing our own name, building our own kingdom, and seeking our own will. It reminds us that our material possessions have not come by dint of our own initiative, industry, or ingenuity. It points to our own lack of righteousness and need of pardon. It also warns against trusting our invincibility to conquer temptation.

Jesus prayed for significant matters. He never asked for trivial items. All five petitions deal with meaningful matters. Four of the five relate to spiritual issues. One (for daily bread) pertains to a material want, which shows the legitimacy of bringing physical needs to our Father in prayer. But with 80% of the petitions dealing with spiritual subjects, is not our Lord trying to teach us to pray primarily for spiritual topics?

Later when Paul prayed for various churches, he majored in requests for the spiritual maturity of believers. For example, he wanted the Colossians to be "fill[ed] with the knowledge of his will through all spiritual wisdom and understanding" and to "live a life worthy of the Lord," and to be "strengthened with all power" (1:9–11). Not a request about jobs, mortgages, operations, or tests, all certainly permissible. But when a prayer meeting concentrates 80% on bunions, gall bladders, fenders, and finances, can we assert we are praying Jesus' way?

Andrew Murray, author of the classic, *With Christ in the School of Prayer,* was once the chief speaker at an annual convention of the Christian Student Movement in South Africa. A missionary recalls the ringing voice of this frail figure, eighty-four years of age, under 100 pounds. One morning the ministers and missionaries were invited to meet with Dr. Murray. He sat with hands folded upon his knees, with glowing face and kindly smile for all. Although the missionary cannot recall a word of the message, this memory stayed with him for decades. "When the company was fully assembled, Dr. Murray quietly said, 'Let us pray.' When he finished, we all knew that we were in the presence of a man of God."

The disciples who asked Jesus to teach them to pray learned their lesson well. When Jesus ascended to heaven what He basically left behind on planet earth was a little prayer meeting. After the Ascension the disciples returned to Jerusalem, went upstairs to the upper room, and "all joined together constantly in prayer. . . ." (Acts 1:12–14). Prayer helped bring Pentecost and 3,000 converts. In the early days of the church the believers devoted themselves to prayer (2:42). To read the book of Acts is to read the story of a series of prayer meetings (e.g., 3:1; 4:23–31; 6:6; 12:5; 13:2–3; 14:23; 16:25). This accounts for the joyful, unstoppable expansion of the early church. They had seen Jesus accomplish the Father's will through prayer. And now, as they carried out the orders of their Master to spread the gospel to Jerusalem, Judea, Galilee and the ends of the earth, prayer was a major factor in its triumphant progress.

Notes
1. G. Campbell Morgan, *The Gospel According to Luke* (Old Tappan, N.J.: Revell, 1931), p. 142.
2. Haddon Robinson, *Jesus' Blueprint For Prayer* (Grand Rapids: Radio Bible Class, 1989), p. 7.
3. *World Almanac* (New York: Pharos, 1992).

CHAPTER 8

Interceding for Others

A successful young businessman was showing his older pastor around his office. Interrupted by long distance calls, the businessman talked with important clients overseas. The pastor left a little downhearted, thinking, "Here's a man half my age with a spacious office, ample staff, and modern gadgetry to communicate all over the globe. And I'm going back to a small office with little equipment to reach around the world." But when he arrived at church, kneeling to pray, suddenly the thought hit him, "I don't need a big office, nor a fax, nor a staff, nor any electronic apparatus to talk to God. Without leaving my study I can intercede for Christians anywhere and everywhere."

Intercessory prayer was practiced in all ages. Abraham begged the Lord to save Sodom from destruction (Gen. 18:20–33). Job intervened for his miserable comforters (42:7–9). Moses pled for the Israelites who had worshiped a golden calf (Ex. 32:11–13, 31–32). Paul selflessly mediated for his people (Rom. 9:3).

Petition is asking for yourself; intercession is asking in behalf of others. Jesus often prayed to His Father in the interest of a third party, as on the cross for His tormentors. Jesus' intercessory work is foreshadowed in Aaron's breastplate, inset with twelve precious stones, each engraved with a name of one of the tribes. As Aaron bore those names into the Holy of Holies, so today Jesus carries the names of His own into the presence of God. Prayer is now a principle occupation of the ascended Jesus. Says Hebrews,

"Therefore he is able to save completely those who come to God through him, because he always lives to intercede for them" (7:25). Because of His continuous presence before the throne in our behalf, no accuser can successfully bring a charge against us. He is the Lawyer who never lost a case. Someone wrote:

> The Lord Jesus is still praying.
> He ever lives to pray us through.
> Thirty years of living,
> Three years of serving,
> One tremendous act of dying,
> Nineteen hundred years of praying!
> What an emphasis on prayer.

Two examples of Jesus' intercession during His earthly ministry were (1) His prayer for Peter, and (2) His High Priestly Prayer for the disciples.

Interceding for Peter (Luke 22:31–32)

During the Last Supper, Jesus told Peter of a prayer He had made on His behalf at an earlier time. This is the only instance of Jesus revealing an item from His private prayer life.

Why Jesus prayed for Peter. Jesus was aware of a battle raging in the unseen world. The devil, a fearful enemy, the accuser of the brethren, was launching an attack against all the disciples, but especially Peter. The Devil had already conquered Judas, and was boldly seeking the downfall of the others with their leader, Peter, as top target. So Jesus warned Peter, in effect, that the same Devil who had slandered Job was out to get him. "Simon, Simon, Satan has asked to sift you (plural, all) as wheat. But I have prayed for you" (shifting to the singular). Jesus prayed for all the disciples, but now singled out Peter who, because of greater presumption and braggadocio, was in greater danger. Jesus, by using Peter's old name, "Simon, Simon," was reminding him of his fickle nature.

The verb used of Satan's asking expresses a strong desire. *The Pulpit Commentary* imagines the evil one arguing in the presence of God thus, "These chosen ones who are appointed to work in the future so tremendous a work in thy Name, are utterly unworthy. Let me just try to lure them away with my lures. Lo, they will surely fall. See, one has already."[1] But though Satan was doing some powerful asking, Jesus was offering even more forceful praying. In our day, we may be oblivious to the great spiritual battles waging in the unseen world. "Deliver us from the evil one" is a very relevant prayer.

What Jesus prayed for. Though we do not have the full, precise quote of Jesus' prayer, the items requested are easily identifiable. "But I have prayed for you, Simon, that your faith may not fail. And when you have turned back, strengthen your brothers." Jesus prayed for two things: for the preservation of Peter's faith, and for his future usefulness. It was not a vague, "God bless Peter," but specific petitions and to the point. Because Jesus prayed, Peter was restored after his fall to an ongoing ministry.

Peter's preservation. Peter should have been jolted to attention by the mention of Jesus praying for him. This pointed to some sort of danger. But the warning failed to pierce Peter's self-sufficiency. He insisted he was willing to go to prison, even death, for Jesus. Then Jesus predicted, "before the rooster crows today, you will deny three times that you know me." Peter, the first of the disciples to confess the deity of Jesus, believed more in his own strength than in the word of the Lord. That night Peter denied the Lord exactly as predicted. When reminded of the depths of His defection by the cock-crowing around 3 a.m., he went out and wept bitterly.

In spite of his denial Peter was basically loyal. His faith did not fail, nor his love, but his courage did. Jesus didn't pray that Satan should not be allowed to test Peter, but that Peter's faith would not fail. Peter would tumble, but he would not stay down. He would not disintegrate completely, nor fall away fully and finally, but would rise from his relapse. However, until restored by Jesus, probably in a private meeting on the resurrection morn (1 Cor.15:5), Peter must have died a thousand deaths as he remorsefully thought of his gross infidelity. Why didn't he go out and hang himself? How a man so impetuous as Peter ever escaped the fate of Judas, who sought out a tree and hanged himself, remains a mystery of grace, explained mainly by Jesus' intercession. Satan sought to mess up Peter's life but Jesus fervently interceded, and His prayer blocked the potentially ruinous consequences of Peter's stumbling.

Our disloyalty pains Jesus, but if we possess true faith, our faults will be followed by repentance and His ready pardon. We have a Friend at God's right hand who pleads our case.

Peter's future usefulness. Jesus knew how fervently Peter could love, how faithfully he could serve, and how ably he could encourage. Penitence could lead to ministry. His restoration could result in the service of establishing others. So Jesus prayed, "When you have turned back, strengthen your brothers."

Peter became a great exhorter. His example of repentance was an inspiration to his fellow-disciples who had also denied Jesus. He preached the persuasive sermon at Pentecost. He stood as a bulwark of the early church. The first part of Acts is the story of Peter's firm leadership. How frequently words similar to these occur, "And Peter, filled with the Holy Spirit, stood up and said . . ." His boldness amazed the religious leaders. Clay became rock. His influence reaches us centuries later as we read his first epistle, "Clothe yourselves with humility toward one another, . . . Humble yourselves, therefore, under God's mighty hand, that he may lift you up in due time. . . . Be self-controlled and alert. Your enemy the Devil prowls around like a roaring lion looking for someone to devour. Resist him . . ." (1 Pet. 5:5–9).

If we have experienced the grace of God after the shame of failure, we should be better equipped to minister to our brothers and sisters who may need our sympathy. Is it not our duty to strengthen those in the body of Christ who need reestablishment?

What caused Peter's faith to survive, and his usefulness to continue—the simple fact of Jesus praying. The verb used of Jesus' praying for Peter is unusual, the only time used of His praying in the Gospels. It means to want, desire, long for, beg, make supplication, pray. It has the idea of petitioning, asking for a need. Jesus accomplished things through prayer—by asking.

Interceding for His Disciples—His High Priestly Prayer (John 17)

The longest continuous, quoted prayer of Jesus fills an entire chapter. Commonly called the High Priestly Prayer, many think it deserves to be termed the Lord's Prayer more than the one that now bears that title. It was uttered after the Passover meal, in the presence of the disciples as they made their way toward Gethsemane (John 18:1). Along the path the disciples had been listening to His rich discourses. Some suggest their route took them by the temple court with its ornament of the vine and branches, prompting the lesson on that topic in John 15:1–8. After He finished His teaching, they heard Him pray (1) for Himself, (2) for His immediate apostles, (3) and for all future believers.

His Prayer for Himself (1–5)

Jesus "looked toward heaven and prayed" (v. 1). The verb "prayed" is not a usual word for praying, but the simple verb "said." Literally it is "Jesus said." Neither is the verb for prayer in v. 9, 15, and 20 a usual word for praying, but the simple verb "ask." Jesus' praying seems to be played down in John's Gospel (e.g., the prayer episode in Gethsemane is entirely omitted). This downplay of prayer fits the portrait John paints in his Gospel of Jesus as God. In John's record Jesus speaks to the Father as an equal, rather than supplicating as a servant. This High Priestly Prayer seems more like communion than petition—a conference between God the Father and God the Son.

Jesus requests to be glorified. He makes the request twice: "Glorify your Son" (v. 1); then "Glorify me" (v. 5). His request may sound selfish, but its purpose is far from self-seeking. He prays to be glorified so that He may glorify His Father (v. 1). The hour had come for the Son's crucifixion and resurrection. Through these acts of redemption (the prayer speaks as though those events have been completed) the Son will give eternal life to all believers and also increasing knowledge concerning the Father and Son. Jesus is praying for enabling to perform the job for which He had been sent. By fulfilling His task He will bring glory to the Father.

With mission accomplished, the Son requests a rightful restoration of His own pre-existent glory which He enjoyed with the Father prior to creation. When Jesus came to earth, He surrendered, among other things, the outer manifestation of His splendor. Now He wants to return to heaven, so asks, "Father, Glorify me in your presence with the glory I had with you before the world began."

This section of the prayer reveals a high level of the self-

THE MASTER'S PLAN OF PRAYER

consciousness of Jesus as to His person, position, pre-existence, sacrifice on the cross, and return to His rightful place of glory at the right hand of the Father. This first part of the prayer is basic to the rest. Without the answer to this request, the two following sections would be impossible—there would be no disciples nor future believers for whom to pray.

His Prayer for His Immediate Disciples (6–19)

Jesus moves from asking for Himself to entreating for His immediate disciples, the Twelve, or more accurately the Eleven, for Judas had left to make arrangements for the betrayal. Jesus is specifically praying for these apostles, not the world. It doesn't mean that He never prays for the world, but on this occasion He is making requests for His close band of followers. He has two requests: (1) for their protection, and (2) for their sanctification. Does this section suggest how Jesus may have interceded for Peter when He prayed for Him individually?

Their protection (6–16). The disciples are a special group. They are well prepared, given to Jesus by the Father, recipients of and obedient to a large amount of teaching, and believers in the truth that Jesus came from God. So chosen and taught, they were well qualified to carry out the missionary task. But Jesus will soon be leaving them, and they will be going out into a hostile world that threatened to engulf them, despite Jesus' painstaking labors to sharpen and mature them. Jesus' request seems intense. The whole enterprise could flop unless they are protected. The thrust of Jesus entreaty is contained in v. 11, "I will remain in the world no longer, but they are still in the world, and I am coming to you. Holy Father, protect them by the power of your name . . . so that they may be one as we are one."

Up to then Jesus has guarded the disciples. None had been lost except the one doomed to destruction" (v. 12). He does not ask for them to be removed out of the world, but to be protected in an evil world. The future of the church depends upon their faithfulness. So Jesus commits them to His Father's keeping.

Also, knowing the evil propensities of these men, so prone to envy, ambition, and petty strife, all of which have flared so often, Jesus prayed for their unity "that they may be one."

Their sanctification (17–19). Jesus' request, "Sanctify them" is not so much a prayer for holiness or separation from evil as a request for setting them apart for service, just as priests, buildings, and vessels were in Old Testament times. It's a prayer for the consecration of these chosen messengers to their mission of proclaiming the truth. The revelation of truth given the Son by the Father was not only the sphere of their preaching but also the instrument of their consecration. The full sentence reads, "Sanctify them by the truth; your word is truth" (v. 17). The Word of God enshrines the instruction that helps us put off the evil habits of the old life and put on the godly practices of the new life. Saturation in the Scriptures, including reading, searching, meditation, and application provides great protection for going out into the world.

Jesus said He sanctified Himself, not that He had any evil in His life to overcome, for He was sinless. But He dedicated Himself to finishing His task—Calvary loomed before Him on the next day. His sanctification would be a powerful motive for their ministry. "As you sent me into the world, I have sent them into the world. For them I sanctify myself, that they too may be truly sanctified" (v. 19).

His Prayer for All Future Believers (20–26)

Jesus broadens His prayer to include not only His immediate band, but all His followers in the centuries to come. His prayer is twofold: (1) for the unity of all believers, and (2) for their future fellowship in glory.

Their unity (20–23). The unity of believers of all walks and times refers to something deeper than organizational unity or the ecumenical movement. Jesus was contemplating a spiritual unity like that between Father and Son, and between believers and Christ, and through Christ with the Father (vv. 21–23). This prayer was answered on the Day of Pentecost when the Holy Spirit baptized all believers into the one body of Christ (1 Cor. 12:13). And down through the centuries the Holy Spirit has continued to place every new believer into union with the other members of the body. Paul, Luther, Calvin, Tyndale, and Moody would all have found a central core of unity had they lived at the same time in history. The fruit of the Spirit in the lives of believers—love, gentleness, longsuffering, patience, and meekness—would help them keep the unity of the Spirit through the bond of peace (Eph. 4:3).

Christians have not always demonstrated unity. Sometimes churches have been known for their factions, feuds, and fracases. Ecclesiastical fights have often brought the cause of Christ into disrepute, but on the other hand, the display of unity has witnessed to the divine source of the Christian message and to love of God for mankind.

Jesus prayed, "May they be brought to compete unity to let the world know that you sent me and have loved them even as you have loved me" (v. 23). Did not Jesus say a few minutes earlier in the upper room, "All men will know that you are my disciples if you love one another" (13:35). Unity has an indirect evangelistic appeal. Here Jesus did not pray directly for the salvation of unbelievers. Rather He prayed for believers to so display love in their midst that some in the world might be convinced of the truth of the gospel.

Their future fellowship in glory (24–25). Though the world does not know the Father, Jesus restates that He has made the Father known to His disciples and will continue to make known the Father's love. He prays that some day all who belong to Him will fellowship with Him and each other in heaven to contemplate His pre-incarnate glory which He had with the Father.

How sobering to realize that Jesus prayed for *us* in His prayer the night before He died. Nineteen centuries before we were born, He was eager for our security, unity, sanctification, and future fellowship in glory. And He's still praying for us. Perhaps even today He has seen you in danger of some dire Satanic attack and has pled for your safety before the Father's throne.

Practical Suggestions for our Practice of Intercession

Conscientious Christians are often overwhelmed by endless requests for intercession. Dr. Stephen Olford suggests dividing the requests into seven groups, one for each day of the week, with each group connected alliteratively with one of the days. On Sunday, pray for sinners; Monday, missionaries; Tuesday, tasks; Wednesday, workers; Thursday, thanks; Friday, family; and

Saturday, saints. We follow this outline, but making Thursday for the troubled.

Sunday—Sinners. Ceil Rosen, wife of Moishe Rosen, founder of *Jews for Jesus*, became interested in the gospel prior to her husband. But she knew that confessing Christ could disrupt family relationships. She wanted to talk to someone but didn't know where to turn. On a snowy day in 1953 Mrs. Hannah Wago, a missionary, knocked on their door. Some Christian lady, totally unaware of Ceil's search, had asked the missionary to visit the Rosens. Ceil later discovered that this lady's family had been praying three times daily for four years that the Rosens would come to know Jesus as their Messiah. During those years that family had never felt moved to ask a missionary to visit the Rosens—not until Ceil prayed that God would send someone.

Mrs. Wago began teaching every week, but Moishe wanted no part of Ceil's growing interest. Finally he told Ceil that Mrs. Wago was not welcome in their home. Ceil shifted their Bible studies to the telephone. One day Moishe came home to find Ceil engaged in one of their phone Bible studies. Moishe, who ordinarily would not deny Ceil anything, became so infuriated that he ripped the phone out of the wall. Ceil discreetly continued her studies with Mrs. Wago. Eventually Moishe capitulated to the Messiah, later to start *Jews for Jesus*. But the Rosen conversions began with someone praying for them.

Strangely, the Bible does not contain many verses to pray for the salvation of sinners, perhaps taking the practice for granted. But we do have a strong command to pray for workers to go into the harvest. Someone said, "Talking to men for God is a great thing, but talking to God for men is greater still." Few are converted apart from someone's praying.

Monday—Missionaries. Dr. and Mrs. V. Raymond Edman, while missionaries in northern Ecuador, heard of a tribe of such fierce killers that no one had been able to bring them the gospel. The Edmans prayed that someone would reach them. Years later, as President of Wheaton College, Dr. Edman learned the shocking news that five American missionaries had been brutally slain by a tribe of little-known Indians in the heart of Ecuador. It was the tribe for whom the Edmans had prayed. Interestingly, some of those martyred missionaries had been trained at Wheaton College.

Later, several Aucas were won to Christ, including some of those who speared the missionaries. Then Dr. Edman learned that the Auca believers were praying for him. Dr. Edman wrote an article, "For Years I Prayed for Them, Now They Pray for Me."

Most missionary societies publish some type of information sheet, listing matters that need prayerful attention. A missionary wrote this: "Missionaries need intercessors more than admirers. They need prayers more than donors. They live and work in the enemy's territory and become the special object of Satan's attack. Pray for their protection, their power in life and ministry, their flexibility in relationships, an attitude of servanthood, compatibility with fellow-workers, a heart of love for all men, boldness in preaching, fruitfulness in service, filling with the Holy Spirit, an understanding of culture, a discipline in devotional life, proficiency in the use of language, patience with others, safety in travel, courage in danger and loneliness, health in soul and body, wisdom, openness to God's leading, family home life, and children in school."

Tuesday—Tasks. Wesley Duewel in his book, *Touch The World Through Prayer,* says, "Every Christian ministry needs a burden-bearing team of prayer warriors. The effectiveness of any such ministry will depend upon the godliness of the team and the power of prayer that is marshaled behind it. Blessed is that person or ministry that has not only enlisted the aid of prayer partners but has intercessor-watchmen who carry a continual burden for the ministry."[2]

Edith Schaeffer tells how at the beginning of their ministry in Switzerland about twenty people on their own volition promised to pray a certain length of time each day. She credits their faithful intercession for the worldwide influence of L'Abri.

When Francis Schaeffer was diagnosed with cancer, he was preparing the film series, *Whatever Happened to the Human Race?* Associates earnestly prayed for strength for him to complete it.

Filming on several locations, including Israel, Schaeffer would rise at 2 or 3 a.m. each morning, weak and with tired legs, and with cancer raging through his system would say, "I can't do it," and then minutes later would say, "Well, it is only one more day, and it won't be my strength, but His strength." Later, when the film was finished, in the midst of chemotherapy and the additional pain of shingles, he was given strength a day at a time to speak at twenty-one seminars for the film series.[3]

Every gospel-preaching church and parachurch group stands in the need of intercessory prayer. Why not pick out a few, then plead their ministry before the throne?

Wednesday—Workers. Not only missionaries and ministries, but evangelists, broadcasters, pastors, church staffs, Sunday school teachers, executives of Christian organizations, and many other evangelical leaders stand in constant need of prayer.

In the early years of Billy Graham's ministry, a great grandmother in her 70's traveled over 50,000 miles, mostly by bus, to twenty-one crusades. A little known, unofficial member of the Graham team, she would rent a hotel room and rise at 5 a.m. to devote herself to prayer. Before meetings she would go to the empty auditorium and pray for the pulpit, the empty chairs, and the people who would later sit there. *Christian Life* magazine reported that the beginning of her prayer ministry coincided with Graham's emergence as a nationally known figure.[4] Graham is the first to acknowledge that the thousands of prayer partners all over the world compose the "secret weapon" behind his success as an evangelist.

Richard Foster wrote that after completing a major book on prayer he had difficulty praying. Three friends promised to pray for him. For a week Foster stopped praying and spent an hour jogging. At the end of the week he was eager to pray again.

Thursday—Trouble. When Code 99 blares over a hospital's loudspeaking system, immediately a medical team rushes to the patient's room, begins emergency treatment, and works intensely against time to save life. Similarly, when the Lord permits a crisis, we should immediately marshal our intercessors. This is why many churches and groups have prayer chains.

The biweekly letter *Perspective* suggests that the daily newspaper can serve as a prayer list for those in trouble. Tragedy on its pages can lead us to pray for the victims. Someone's house burns. A flood inundates a home. Two teenagers are critically injured in a car accident. Street children in the cities of Brazil. The starving of Africa. The poor. The homeless. Those wounded in war. Addicts. The sick, the shut-in, the hospitalized. The elderly. The blind. Abused children. The unemployed. The mentally ill. The plague of cancer.

The scourge of AIDS. Those suffering from Alzheimer's. Praying will be more meaningful if we personalize it.

Friday—Family. Parents brought infants to Jesus for His blessing. He took them in His arms and prayed. Through the centuries parents have beseeched God for the salvation and usefulness of their children. A missionary doctor in Ivory Coast, walking me along the path from his house to his hospital, pointed out several trees. "I gave each tree the name of one of my children, and I pray for each child as I pass his or her tree to and from work morning and evening." One U.S. pastor prays for his children and grandchildren on his daily morning walk. Augustine's mother Monica prayed for her wayward son's salvation and ultimately saw him surrender to Christ. The night I accepted Jesus, my mother told me that she had prayed for that night before I was born.

Pat Williams said that it dawned on him that he had a disciplined prayer life for his sports and missionary efforts, but not "for his wife on a daily basis. He put a sign near his office phone, 'Have you prayed for Jill today?' Praying for her throughout the day helped create a spiritual bond that had never been there before."[5]

More often, it's a wife that prays for her husband. A newlywed, married to a fine Christian, was shocked to discover pornographic magazines under their mattress. Through tears she asked the Lord to show her how to handle this. Confronted in a loving way, he tearfully said, "I have a problem. I've had it since eighth grade." That night she watched him burn the magazines and prayerfully hand his problem over to the Lord. Though the problem has gone, they both know that Satan will attack again, so she prays for a hedge of protection around her husband.

Jesus' brothers did not believe on Him before His death. Surely He prayed for them. Acts tells us that they were among the believers in the upper room before Pentecost. Brother James became the leader of the church at Jerusalem (Acts 15:13–21).

Countless family members have been brought into the kingdom through the prayers of relatives. Dr. V. Gilbert Beers, former editor of *Christianity Today,* told how his wife's grandmother, whom he had never met, had shaped the lives of all members of her family for four generations. Suddenly widowed, expecting the birth of her fourth child, totally penniless, and with no way to make a living, she moved in with her brother. In her nothingness she decided that her mission in life would be to pray for the salvation and spiritual growth of her four children and her unborn descendents. Believing her prayers would be answered, she devoted the rest of her life to her mission. Beers reports that all four of her children reflected the presence of Christ in their lives. All seventeen in his wife's generation were dedicated to Christ, and established Christian families. The same for the fourth generation. Through the years many entered full-time Christian service. All of grandma's descendants look on her as the source of a great heritage.

Saturday—Saints. One February a letter came, "I picked a card from the top of my pile of Christmas cards and it was yours! That means that today is my special day to pray for you." The note came from the parents of a martyred missionary who remember their friends in prayer by going through their Yuletide cards.

Believers need to pray for fellow-believers, especially new converts. Instead of critically scrutinizing babes in Christ, we should surround them with loving intercession. An Australian Bible teacher, visiting an American church leader, remarked that several outstanding Christian laymen in Australia had been converted when the American prelate led revival campaigns in Australia twenty-seven years before. The American's face lit up. "Can you give me any of their names." After a minute the Australian proceeded to name half a dozen. Through moist eyes the American said, "During those campaigns I asked the counselors for a list of the young people who made decisions. I have prayed daily for that list for twenty-seven years, and I recognize some of the names you have mentioned."

We know that Paul prayed for the saints at Rome, Corinth, Ephesus, Philippi, Colosse, and Thessalonica. When Dr. Moseley was president of Nyack Missionary College, he kept on his desk a list of all the students and prayed for them by name regularly. A pastor prayed through his list of several hundred members at least once every month. How wonderful to have secret prayer pals! Do you have a list for whom you pray systematically? Intercession is a way of loving and helping others.

We need not spend hours in prayer every day to qualify for

God's prayer army. Thanks for those who can and do. But He does wish us to add the dimension of intercession to our prayer life. After all, we are a kingdom of priests (Rev. 1:6).

Notes
1. *The Pulpit Commentary,* Luke, vol. 11, p. 201.
2. Wesley Duewel, *Touch the World Through Prayer* (Grand Rapids: Zondervan, 1986), p. 83.
3. Edith Schaeffer, *The Life of Prayer* (Wheaton: Crossway, 1992), pp. 32–33, 44.
4. *Christian Life,* August 1962, p. 34.
5. *Rekindled,* p. 133.

CHAPTER 9

Getting "No" for an Answer

A statue of Abraham Lincoln on his knees, possibly the only one of the emancipator sculptured in the attitude of prayer, may be seen in the Washington (D.C.) Cathedral. The inspiration for Herbert Spencer Houck's work came from his grandfather who, one day walking through the fields near Gettysburg, discovered Lincoln kneeling in the leaves. The recollection of this oft-repeated story led Houck to fashion "Lincoln in Prayer."

In Gethsemane Jesus prayed on His knees (Luke 22:39–40). Though He probably knelt often, this is the only time kneeling is mentioned. God can hear our prayers no matter our posture. But it may not be a bad idea to pray on our knees from time to time.

A crowd of two thousand politicians, business executives, and notables gathered at the Washington (D.C.) Hilton ballroom in January 1991 for the annual Leadership Conference. With the Gulf War two weeks old, Dr. Charles Stanley, Atlanta pastor and TV speaker, preached fervently on the need for America to humble itself before God. Toward the end of his message he asked, "What would happen if two thousand people got on their knees, humbled themselves before God, and cried out for forgiveness?" After a few more hints the crowd realized that he was serious about getting them on their knees in their Brooks Brothers suits and Florsheim shoes. He asked those physically able to join him on his knees and pray until the moderator thought the time was over. With that, Stanley turned and dropped from sight. The ballroom became silent. Then a gentle shuffle of chairs, as most of the crowd followed his lead. A devout air filled the ballroom.

Kneeling may be uncomfortable and undignified, but it helps humility. It says, "Lord, I acknowledge that You are the Master." Kneeling narrows our field of vision and reduces distractions. Tradition says that Jesus' brother James, leader of the church at Jerusalem, prayed so often on his knees that they became hardened like those of a camel.

The kneeling posture in Gethsemane reflected some of Jesus' agony. But His anguish went far beyond kneeling. Artists often miss the intensity of His emotional strain by depicting a serene Jesus on His knees beside a big rock, in white robe, with folded hands and peaceful face, a light from heaven shining on His hair. The Gospels picture Him painfully overcome with intense distress.

That Jesus could experience such anxiety so soon after the triumph expressed in the closing sentences of His High Priestly Prayer is puzzling. The prayer ends with the anticipation of Jesus reunited in heaven with all His disciples viewing the glory which He shared with His Father from before the creation of the world. John, the only Gospel which records the High Priestly Prayer, proceeds directly to the account of Jesus' arrest in the garden and skips the garden episode. The omission of the garden agony by John fits his purpose of emphasizing the deity of Jesus. The inclusion of the garden agony by the three other Gospel writers stresses the dual nature of Jesus, indeed a Man of Sorrows, fully man as well as fully God.

The Anguish

After celebrating the Passover and finishing His High Priestly Prayer, Jesus led the Eleven, Judas absent, toward the Mount of Olives. They crossed the brook Kidron and entered an olive grove, a favorite place of prayer for their Master. Today centuries-old large olive trees give the garden an authentic ring. Jesus told His disciples, "Sit here while I go yonder and pray." A usual word for prayer is used. But taking with Him the inner three, Peter, James, and John, Jesus began to experience a level of sorrow more oppressive than any He had ever known.

Matthew says that Jesus began to be sorrowful and troubled

(Matt. 26:37). "Sorrowful" signifies grief as when a loved one dies. "Troubled," a potent word, means distracted, disturbed, in a state of confusion following shock. Mark says Jesus was deeply distressed (14:33), implying a sudden terror or trauma. Both Matthew (26:38) and Mark (14:34) say He was *exceedingly* sorrowful, even to the point of death. The writer of Hebrews was likely thinking of Gethsemane when he wrote, "During the days of Jesus' life on earth, he offered up prayers and petitions with loud cries and tears to the one who could save him from death, and he was heard because of his reverent submission" (5:7). In the garden He drank bitterness to its acrid depths.

Leaving the three disciples, Jesus went a stone's throw beyond, fell with His face to the ground and in His anguish prayed, "My Father, if it is possible, may this cup be taken from me. Yet not as I will, but as you will" (Matt. 26:39). Returning to the disciples, He found them sleeping. He said, with Peter especially in mind, "Could you men not keep watch with me for one hour?" (26:40).

Again exhorting them to watch and pray, He went a second time and prayed, "My Father, if it is not possible for this cup to be taken away unless I drink it, may your will be done" (26:42). As He approached the limits of His endurance, "An angel from heaven appeared to him and strengthened him" (Luke 22:43). Despite this help at the height of the struggle, Luke says, "Being in anguish, he prayed more earnestly, and his sweat was like drops of blood falling to the ground" (22:44). Rising from prayer and returning to the disciples, He found them heavy with sleep. So He left them and once more went away and prayed the third time. Returning the third time, He said, "Are you still sleeping and resting? Look, the hour is near, and the Son of Man is betrayed into the hands of sinners. Rise, let us go! Here comes my betrayer" (22:45–46). Then came His arrest by a band of soldiers, led by Judas.

Picture that lonely figure in the garden, flat on the earth, face smudged with tears and dirt, hair mussed with sweat, cheeks spotted with blood. This was a tempest, not tranquillity.

What a spectacle—the Prince of Peace, disturbed and destitute of peace! Is this the One who is the strength of the feeble and the shield of the distressed? He is—and because of His Gethsemane experience He is all the more qualified to help us in

THE MASTER'S PLAN OF PRAYER

our weaknesses. As our High Priest at the Father's right hand He is able to sympathize with us, inviting all who are weary and burdened, "Come to me, . . . and I will give you rest" (Matt. 11:28).

Reasons for His Anguish

We stand on holy ground when we explore the reasons for Jesus' agony. Some suggest that He was shrinking from the hideous suffering awaiting Him. Certainly death by crucifixion was one of the most gruesome methods of execution ever devised by cruel men. Historians and physicians have vividly described its lingering torture. But the real agony was not physical pain, which through the centuries many have bravely faced, but that anguish which stemmed from the war waging within His soul and related to the meaning of the Cross.

What were the contents of the cup from which He shrank and which would cause so much suffering?

He was seeing more clearly the horror of sin. In that cup was clustered all the sin of the human race from the day of Adam's disobedience—all the depravity of every person who ever inhabited this planet—every rebellion against God's majestic holiness. Many can recall the inner pain when first convicted of sin by the Holy Spirit, including the many sleepless nights before experiencing the joy of forgiveness. Others come more progressively to realize the exceeding sinfulness of sin. But however we come to see how ghastly our own individual sin is, how abhorrent it must have been for Jesus to face the prospect of drinking the abominable cup of our universal collective iniquity!

Jesus was about to be made sin for us. The righteous, spotless Son of God was soon to have placed on Him all the sins of all mankind. Imagine an immaculate housewife, forced by circumstances to move out of her spotless home to live in a filthy house, full of cobwebs and rolling dustballs. She who hated dirt now surrounded by dirt. Jesus, the essence of purity, was about to be covered with the totality of human evil.

He was beginning to identify with the role of Mediator. He not only saw more clearly the horror of sin, but He now saw Himself as the Sin-bearer. He beheld the Father about to lay on Him the iniquity of us all. He viewed Himself about to be wounded for our transgressions. At this hour heaven was beginning to look on Him as standing in the sinner's stead to be treated the way a sinful creature rightly deserved. He sensed that He was the substitute, accepted by divine justice to bear our load of divine wrath. The cup was often used figuratively in the Old Testament for God's wrath (Ps. 75:8). Jesus was about to become the Scapegoat on which the sins of the people were symbolically placed, and which was then driven into the wilderness on the Day of Atonement.

He felt the Father beginning to withdraw His presence. Jesus, the Son of God, who had been loved from eternity by the Father, and who had turned to His Father in every crisis, was about to be abandoned by His Father. The eclipse of His Father's presence began to close in on His soul as He knelt in the garden. The One who had previously cheered His spirit was leaving Him to single-handedly contend for the deliverance of mankind.

Hell involves separation from God. On the cross Jesus would somehow suffer the equivalent of a lost eternity, concentrated into those hours in which He paid the penalty for our sins, making Him cry out in the awful darkness, "My God, my God, why have you forsaken me?" A foretaste of that desolation, alienated from the others in the Trinity for the only occasion in time or eternity, began to grip Him there in the garden.

So many ask, "Is Jesus the only way to God? Are there not many roads to heaven?" Does not Jesus' struggle give us the answer? Had there been any other way, the Father would have let His Son escape. But the Lamb had to die—alone, forsaken.

He suffered attack by Satan. An hour or so earlier Jesus had said, "The prince of this world is coming" (John 14:30). A greater temptation than suffered in the forty days in the wilderness, this became Jesus' fiercest struggle, a hand-to-hand combat with Satan. Perhaps Satan hissed, "See, You have no friends. Your Father will forsake You. The soldiers are on the way to seize You. Soon You'll be on the cross, Your hands fastened by nails. And Your disciples—behold them asleep. In a few minutes they'll be forsaking and denying You."

And then, "But You can escape." Pointing back to the entrance of the garden, Satan might have suggested, "Why don't You walk out, make a left turn and You can avoid it all—the cross and all the agony." Looking through the olive trees in the moonlight, Jesus could see Jerusalem. And not far away in the other direction a path that led to Bethany, the home of Mary and Martha. They would give Him a welcome and a refuge. Or He could slip into the wilderness of Jericho and hide for months or years.

The Prayer

It was a *customary* prayer; it was His habit to pray in this favorite spot when in the Jerusalem area (Luke 22:39).

It was a *humble* prayer; He fell to His knees.

It was a *sorrowful* prayer; He wept under the burden.

It was a *lonely* prayer; His disciples fell asleep, failing to watch with Him in His crucial need of companionship.

It was a *persevering* prayer; Jesus used virtually the same words in all three prayers. When Jesus spoke against repetition in prayer, He did not mean that repetition itself was wrong, only when recited mechanically or as a magic formula. He spoke often of persistence in prayer. Keep on asking, and it shall be given you. Keep on seeking, and ye shall find. Keep on knocking, and it shall be opened to you. He told of the poor widow who kept bothering the unjust judge till he heard her case. He taught that we ought always to pray and not faint. Now He practiced importunity. When no answer came the first time, He prayed a second time, and a third. Only then did peace prevail, creating calm to face the storm. John Calvin wrote, "We must repeat the same supplications not twice or three times only, but as often as we have need, a hundred and a thousand times. . . . We must never weary in waiting for God's help."[1]

It was an *earnest* prayer. What groans! What tears! Even blood! Luke records, "And being in anguish, He prayed more earnestly (22:44). "Earnestly" is a pictorial word, literally, "stretched-out-ed-ly." "Intensely" might be more accurate. Spiritual warfare often requires the price of wrestling in prayer. If, like the disciples, we were asked to pray for an hour, would we discover that we too would rather sleep, unable to overcome our self-centeredness for sixty minutes?

It was more than an hour-long prayer period. When Jesus found the disciples asleep the first time, His rebuke was,

"Could you not watch with Me one hour?" Since He prayed two more segments, the total time may well have been two or more hours.

Dick Eastman, founder and executive director of Change the World Ministries, says that with the gift of twenty-four hours every day believers should be challenged to use one of them in prayer and Bible study. One hour a day makes 365 hours a year, the equivalent of 45 eight-hour days, an awesome potential for change in the life of a believer and in our world. To those who ask, "How can anyone possibly pray for an hour?" Eastman has written a book, *The Hour That Changes The World*, which suggests breaking the hour into twelve five-minute segments: praise, waiting quietly, confession, praying in scriptural language, watching alertly, intercession for others, petition for self, thanksgiving, singing, meditation, listening for God's guidance, and ending with praise again. He suggests applying the plan with "spiritual liberty rather than regimented legality."[2]

An English professor with a busy teaching program, and rarely an evening at home, planned to finish lecture preparation by 9 p.m. one evening in order to watch a particular movie on TV. Rushing through his work and bolting a quick snack, he heard a voice so clearly that he gazed into the darkness of the garden to see who was there. The professor, not given to voices, said it was so unmistakable that he kept looking for the owner. The voice said, "Could you not watch with Me one hour?" Stunned, he was compelled not to switch on the TV, but to go to his study where he spent not one but two hours in meditation on the Word and prayer. He testified that he received spiritual riches that night, wholly undeserved in view of his initial reluctance.

It was a *submissive prayer*. Surprisingly, Jesus didn't get the answer He requested. Surely the Son of God would have met every condition of answered prayer. Practicing known sin blocks the answer (Ps. 66:18); Jesus was sinless. Harboring an unforgiving spirit closes God's ears (Mark 11:25); Jesus maintained a forgiving attitude, even on the cross. Mistreating a wife hinders a husband's prayers (1 Pet. 3:7); Jesus wasn't married. Wavering faith nullifies a prayer (James 1:6–7); Jesus' faith was perfect. Ostentation spoils a prayer (Matt. 6:7); Jesus was without guile. Wrong motives make a request miss God's throne (James 4:3); Jesus was void of selfish thoughts. Praying must harmonize with the will of God (1 John 5:14); herein may be the problem.

Jesus asked for something which was not the Father's will when He prayed to escape the cup. It was not the Father's plan for Him to bypass the cross. Jesus had come to do the Father's will, and submission had been the governing factor all through His ministry. To please the Father, Jesus had left the many mansions of glory to be born of a human mother. On earth He spoke and did only what His Father wanted, even though submission meant poverty, inconvenience, and the ignominious shame of the cross. When the mob derided, "He saved others, but He can't save Himself," they spoke the truth. Since the Father's program required death as the price of man's redemption, Jesus must not save Himself, but rather give Himself a ransom for many. So He prayed, "Not My will, but Thine be done."

God does not give us everything we ask for. He grants us those things in accordance with His character and will. Thus, when we pray, we should be asking for those things that He plans for us. Our prayers should be directed toward the accomplishing of His purposes in the world and in our lives.

George Muller, noted man of prayer, used to mull for days over a subject for prayer, sometimes months, before offering that request, trying to find out if he had the divine mind. Jesus' prayers were controlled by the plan of God. As the divine outline was progressively revealed, He followed it step by step. In the garden He brought His prayer in line with the Father's will, submitting to a divine "no" to His plea to avoid the cross.

The apostle Paul knew what it was to receive a "no." If any Christian was qualified to have his prayers answered, it was Paul. Yet He relates how "there was given to me a thorn in my flesh, a messenger of Satan, to torment me. Three times I pleaded with the Lord to take it away from me. But he said to me, 'My grace is sufficient for you, for my power is made perfect in weakness'" (2 Cor. 12:7–9). The thorn was not removed, but the Lord gave him ample grace to bear it.

Someone remarked that every prayer receives either a "yes," or "wait," or "no." When a request is refused, it may be simply a delay. If decisively denied, it is as truly answered as when it is granted. The Lord is responding, "I have something better for you.

Trust me." Many a happily married person has exclaimed, "How glad I am that the Lord never answered my prayer to marry my teenage crush. It would have been a disaster!" C. S. Lewis wrote, "If God had granted all the silly prayers I've made in my life, where should I be now?"[3]

Edith Schaeffer tells how the weekend after her husband's diagnosis of cancer most of the family gathered in a hotel room near the hospital in Rochester, Minnesota. It "was our private family time of worship and study together. Each of us gave a chapter that meant a great deal to us at the time, and we each prayed. . . . Oh yes, we did pray for more time for Fran. . . ."[4] She continued, noting that the cancer did not go away, "What was the matter with our faith? Oh yes, we prayed, and oh yes, prayer was answered." But in another way. She told how Fran's weakness was dramatically evident, but how during the last three months of his life, twelve times he went straight from the hospital, after blood transfusions, to take part in seminars in different cities.

Amy Carmichael's earliest memory of prayer went back to the age of three when she prayed most earnestly that her brown eyes would be changed to blue, and then early next morning climbed up on a chair to gaze disappointedly into the mirror and see the same brown eyes. Years later, as a missionary to India, she learned of the terrible plight of girls, handed over by their parents to serve as temple prostitutes. Wishing to learn more of this practice firsthand, she disguised herself by darkening her skin, and slipped into several temples to look around. She commented, "If my eyes had been blue, I would never have passed for an Indian." Deeply influenced by these temple surveys, she exercised a ministry which enabled her to rescue thousands of girls from a wretched life.

A Christian physician was treating a little girl who was dying. Though her mother was praying constantly for her daughter's recovery, the little girl's condition grew progressively worse. Finally one evening, during her mother's prayers, the little girl interrupted, "Stop praying for me. I'm tired and I'm ready to die. I'm not afraid." The relief was overwhelming. The mother stopped giving reasons to God for what she wanted, and began asking God's will to be done. In the remaining days of the child's life, the two talked about the daughter's soon departure and what heaven would be like. This allowed the child to die in an atmosphere of love and understanding, which replaced the panic and unreality which previously permeated the home.

A man in the prime of life saw his successful career cut down by cancer. Later he said, "Nothing but just what has happened to me would ever have brought me to my senses and to the Lord." This notation was found after his death, "There is no way of distinguishing between a blessing and a misfortune while it is happening."

An anonymous Confederate soldier wrote this testimony,

> I asked God for strength that I might achieve,
> I was made weak that I might learn humbly to obey.
> I asked for health that I might do greater things,
> I was given infirmity that I might do better things.
> I asked for riches that I might be happy,
> I was given poverty that I might be wise.
> I asked for power that I might have the praise of men,
> I was given weakness that I might feel the power of God.
> I asked for all things that I might enjoy life,
> I was given life that I might enjoy all things.
> I got nothing that I asked for—but everything I hoped for.
> Almost despite myself, my unspoken prayers were answered.
> I am, among all men, most richly blessed.

The Answer

Jesus' prayer in the garden was a *triumphant* prayer. When He prayed that God's will be done, the greatest battle in world history had been won. Centuries before, in the garden of Eden, the first Adam had blown his relationship with God and dragged the human race into depravity and condemnation. Here, in the garden of Gethsemane, the second Adam had triumphed, guaranteeing the forgiveness of sins and victory over death and the tomb.

What a contrast between Jesus and His disciples! He prayed, but they slept and consequently were unprepared for the crisis ahead. We must watch, pray, and avoid those situations which can blindside us. A prayerless life is a powerless life. But Jesus! Resigning Himself to the Father's will, He rose from the ground and went majestically to face the mob then arriving at the garden entrance to arrest Him.

The disciples, taken by surprise, panicked and fled. Peter did make a feeble attempt to defend Jesus, cutting off the ear of the high priest's servant. Jesus magnanimously healed the servant, commanding Peter, "Put your sword away! Shall I not drink the cup the Father has given me?" (John 18:11). Jesus had won the victory!

Jesus also said, "Do you think I cannot call on my Father, and he will at once put at my disposal more than twelve legions of angels? But how then would the Scriptures be fulfilled that say it must happen in this way?" (Matt. 26:53–54). The prayer for a rescue has been called "the prayer Jesus did not pray." Prayer for escape was not God's will.

What a difference in the emotional state of Jesus when He left the garden from when He entered. Entering, He displayed strong agitation. Leaving, though led away in chains to face the badgering of a nightlong trial and next-day crucifixion, He was the picture of a man in command of the situation. So majestic was his bearing that the officers who came to arrest Him fell backward to the ground when He stated His identity (John 18:2–6). Throughout His ordeal He displayed the essence of tranquillity in a sea of turbulence. Clearly something occurred in the garden to dramatically change His emotional state. Through intense prayer He received an overcoming calm which was displayed through the ensuing flogging, ridicule, and torture. His composed demeanor grew out of His resignation to His Father's will.

Yielding to the Lord is not easy when it means accepting something other than what you have been praying for. The Salvation Army's *War Cry* tells the story of author Dr. Dennis E. Hensley who in 1974 suffered damage to the nerves near his left temple. The result was gross disfigurement to the entire left side of his face, sagging cheek, a left eyelid that would not blink, twisted lips, half of his tongue numb, and a forehead that would not wrinkle on the left side.

He was terrified. Instinctively he prayed fervently for a miraculous recovery. No healing came. After ten days he was transferred from the local hospital to a large university research complex. When a young hospital chaplain stopped by, Hensley told him he had prayed for his face to be healed, but there had been no improvement. The chaplain read the story of Joseph who forgave his brothers for selling him into slavery. When the brothers wondered why he could be so magnanimously unrevengeful, Joseph explained that God had used their evil to work His good, and to make him the second most powerful man in Egypt, thus able to save his brothers in time of famine.

"Now you have a similar opportunity," the chaplain told Hensley. "Life has dealt you a hard blow. Is your faith strong enough for you to stop praying for what you want and instead, discover what good God can bring out of this?"

"But I'm paralyzed," Hensley mumbled through twisted lips.

"Just one side of your face," the chaplain countered. "Your legs, feet, hands, arms, and back work fine. So does your hearing, thinking, seeing, and sense of touch. Find out what God has in store for you. Yield to Him."

From then on Hensley changed his prayer. He continued asking for healing, but he also prayed that if healing were not part of God's will, then he wished for the grace to accept this situation and to serve where the Lord could use him. To his amazement the paralysis turned out to be a blessing. Hensley had to attend speech therapy class to learn how to speak clearly again. He received instruction on vocal projection, enunciation, delivery, and body language. As a result, he now delivers more than eighty major speeches each year at colleges and corporations. He also teaches Sunday school, and makes numerous guest appearances on radio and TV. Had it not been for the paralysis, this phase of his career might never have opened.

Since 1974 he has regained feeling and most of the motor movement in his forehead, nose, lips, and tongue. Though eyelids and left cheek still show evidence of the original nerve damage, he never gives it a thought. If people ask about it, he responds, "It was something that seemed to start out bad, but through the power of prayer it wound up working to my good."

Hensley says that if we ever catch ourselves saying, "I'd pray more if I thought it would do me any good," just change that to, "I'm praying now, Lord, so that I can discover what is good for my life!"[5]

Notes

1. John Calvin, *Sermons on Ephesians* (Edinburgh: Banner of Truth Trust, 1975), p. 683.
2. Dick Eastman, *The Hour That Changes the World* (Grand Rapids: Baker, 1978), p. 10.
3. C. S. Lewis, *Letters to Malcolm* (New York: Harcourt, Brace & World, 1964), p. 28.
4. *The Life of Prayer*, p. 32.
5. Dennis E. Hensley, "The 'Jesus Pattern' of Prayer," *The War Cry*, 8 December 1990.

CHAPTER 10

Forgiving Our Tormentors

When the *S.S. General Meigs* pulled away from dock at San Francisco in December 1948 for Japan, the passenger list included Jacob DeSchazer, his wife, and baby boy. It was DeSchazer's second time to cross the Pacific. On his first tour he went with bombs; the second trip he went with the Bible.

Volunteering for a dangerous mission in World War II, he found himself on board the aircraft carrier *Hornet* with sixteen planes on deck. As part of Jimmy Doolittle's 1942 air raid on Japan, his group flew to Naogoya, 300 miles south of Tokyo, and dropped four incendiary bombs. Flying back, they ran out of gas over China and parachuted into a rice field. He was picked up by Japanese soldiers the next morning and, along with seven other survivors, flown to Tokyo. Then began forty months as a prisoner, thirty-four of which were spent in solitary confinement in China. Three fellow-soldiers were executed; another died of slow starvation.

By this time DeSchazer was very bitter toward his Japanese captors who didn't hide their hatred of him and all Americans. In return, his spirit of revenge nearly drove him insane. Then he recalled that Christians were supposed to love their enemies. He wished for a Bible to read. After two years of asking, his captors brought him a brand new Bible. In June 1944 he came to understand the gospel and experienced the forgiveness of sins. Instead of hatred toward the Japanese, he felt love. He thought,

"They did not know any better. I remembered how Jesus, on the cross, prayed for His tormentors, 'Father, forgive them, for they know not what they do'. I found enough grace to take the same attitude toward my cruel guards." He was released the following year. Two months later he began training for missionary service at Seattle Pacific College. Three years later he left with his wife and baby, his second trip across the Pacific, to proclaim the gospel to the Japanese people.

Jesus' Prayer

Crucifixion is one of the most hideous forms of execution known to the human race. Often the cross was laid flat on the ground, and with the victim held down on it, the soldiers drove a long spike through the wrists and another through the ankles. In the case of Jesus, He had already suffered scourging in which a whip, embedded with pieces of bone, tore open strips of flesh across His back. He had endured the long hours of His trial and had stumbled under the weight of the heavy wooden cross loaded on His sore shoulders. Customarily, after the nailing, the cross was dropped into a prepared hole in the ground with a jolt that would jar every bone in the body. No chaplain, no last meal, no ritual of Psalm reading, no word of comfort.

Victims usually struggled, screamed, shrieked, swore, and spat at their executioners. But not Jesus. Instead, as a lamb before her shearers is dumb, so He opened not His mouth. When He did speak, His words were unbelievably amazing. It was to pray for those who were despitefully persecuting Him. The dumbfounded soldiers heard Him say, "Father, forgive them, for they do not know what they are doing" (Luke 23:34).

Apparently He didn't pray this prayer just once, but kept repeating it. The use of the imperfect tense indicates repeated action. Though some Greek scholars believe the imperfect had lost some of its keen edge at this period, others hold to its significance of continuous action. Dr. A. T. Robertson's *Translation of Luke's Gospel* renders it, "Then Jesus was saying."[1] Helen Barrett Montgomery's *Centenary Translation of the New Testament* plainly puts it, "Jesus kept saying." [2]

As the soldiers crush Him to the ground and hammer in the

nails, hear Him pray, "Father, forgive." As the priests mock Him, hear Him pray, "Father, forgive." As the thieves revile, hear Him pray, "Father, forgive." As the mob ridicules, hear Him pray, "Father, forgive."

This was a prayer of intercession. His own excruciating pain did not make Him forget others. As soon as His blood (the blood of the Lamb of God) began to flow, the great High Priest began His work of intercession. This prayer was the first of seven sayings on the cross. The first three were for others: His tormentors, the repentant thief, and His mother. His own needs, like thirst, came last. Note that He did not pray, "Forgive Me," often the first plea of dying men. He did not ask for forgiveness, for He was sinless. Nor was this a mechanical, formal prayer, but a spontaneous outburst at a moment of crisis.

Jesus was practicing what He preached. His first words on prayer recorded in the New Testament were, "Love your enemies and pray for those who persecute you" (Matt. 5:44). Jesus was now returning good for evil. He held no anger, bitterness, resentment, nor desire for revenge on those mistreating Him. His plea has been called the divinest prayer ever offered.

Jesus shows that we can pray anywhere, even on a cross. Immobilized, hands unable to bless, and feet unable to walk paths of mercy, He prayed. The incapacitated and shut-in can reach out through prayer. More than one revival has been traced to invalids who in their solitude engaged in fervent entreaty.

The cross seems a strange spot to pray. Gethsemane seems the more likely place. Yet it was because Jesus did pray in Gethsemane that He was able to pray on the cross in the way He did. The Hebrew ethic said an eye for an eye and a tooth for a tooth. The Romans practiced revenge, but Jesus begged the Father for forgiveness for His enemies. On what grounds?

The Basis of Jesus' Prayer

Jesus prayed for their forgiveness because "they know not what they are doing." They did understand that they were putting someone to death, but they did not grasp the import of their deed. They did not know the identity of their victim, nor the reason for His death.

This prayer was not a petition for blanket cancellation of the sins of everyone around the cross. A few minutes earlier Jesus had warned the weeping women on the road to Golgotha of coming judgment when people would scream for the mountains to fall on them (Luke 23:28–30). Thrusting pardon indiscriminately on everyone present would have been inconsistent with both mankind's freedom and divine justice. Jesus never forced amnesty on a crowd, but granted forgiveness to individuals on a plea of faith.

Nor should Jesus' prayer be used to justify ignorance as an excuse for breaking the law. If a motorist is caught speeding and pleads ignorance of the speed limit, he is nevertheless guilty and punishable. But Jesus did teach that sins done in ignorance are less serious than sins committed against light. He declared that the residents of Capernaum will find the day of judgment less bearable than the citizens of Sodom because if the miracles done in Capernaum had been performed in Sodom, Sodom would have repented and survived Matt 11:23–24. Paul wrote later that none of the rulers of this age (probably including both Roman and Jewish) understood the wisdom of God imbedded in the gospel, "for if they had, they would not have crucified the Lord of glory" (1 Cor. 2:8). Ignorance does not excuse an offense, but it does seem to lessen its guilt.

If with the passing of time a person who sins in ignorance becomes enlightened as to the error of their way and the true nature of their trespass and repents, their change of heart and new course of conduct will help them avoid future judgment.

Jesus' prayer was a request for delay of judgment. Knowing the longsuffering of His Father, Jesus asked that the execution of the sentence of those participating in the crime of the crucifixion be held in abeyance until they could comprehend the heinousness of what they were doing. It was not an entreaty for a sweeping nullification of the consequences of their guilt, but a supplication for the postponement of punishment justly due them. The verb translated "forgive" also means "suffer" or "permit" and might be paraphrased here, "Father, let be. Don't interfere now. Release them now, for they don't understand the implication of what they are doing."

Jesus was saying, "Hold back the winds of anger from striking

this crowd until the significance of their felony dawns on them."
It was a wonder that that thunderbolts of God's wrath did not
fall immediately and dispatch into eternal damnation every
participant involved in the infamy of crucifying the Lord of Glory.
But judgment did not fall, because Jesus prayed. A forty-year
period of respite was mercifully granted them before the
destruction of Jerusalem and its temple, during which the people
had ample time to reassess the magnitude of their deed and to
turn in repentance to their Messiah.

Don't we often ask why evil people seem to prosper, and why
God lets good people suffer injustice at the hands of wicked men?
We wonder why His judgment doesn't descend immediately on
evildoers? This delay should not lull us into a sense of false security
by thinking that God is winking at sin, for God is not mocked,
and people will reap what they sow, The postponement should
remind us of God's patience. Temporary reprieve does not mean
dismissal of charges. Rather, the interim of deferred penalty
provides a golden chance for repentance. If repentance, then
forgiveness. If hardness of heart, then judgment.

Some believe Jesus' prayer was mainly in behalf of those actually
engaged in the crucifixion, meaning the Roman soldiers for whom
this was just another execution. Maybe they were mercenaries or
captives, forced into this repulsive duty, and hardened by frequent
practice to this barbaric mode of execution. The soldiers, it is
argued, thought they were just putting some criminal to death,
when in reality they were murdering the Messiah, the Son of God,
the Savior of believing mankind.

Those who think that Jesus' prayer was for the soldiers suggest
that in contrast to the soldiers, the Jewish populace knew what
they were doing when they shouted, "Away with Him. We will
not have this man to rule over us." But the New Testament teaches
that the people did *not* know fully, as Peter indicated in preaching
to the crowd at the temple gate after the healing of the lame man,
"You disowned the Holy and Righteous One and asked that a
murderer be released to you. You killed the author of life," adding,
"Now, brothers, I know that you acted in ignorance, as did your
leaders. . . . Repent then, and turn to God, so that your sins may
be wiped out" (Acts 3:13–15, 17, 19). Peter included both leaders
and people as acting in ignorance.

Incidentally, this was one of the rare times that Jesus prayed for unsaved people. His overall emphasis seemed more on praying for workers to go out and evangelize the lost and for believers to display the badge of love toward each other as a convincing testimony to the truth of the gospel.

Results of Jesus' Prayer

A few years ago, Wycliffe missionaries Bruce and Jan Benson with their 14-year-old son Bryan were winding their way down an Andes mountainside. Rounding a hairpin turn, they faced a truckload of people. Immediately rifles pointed at their car. The missionaries recognized them as part of a brutal band of subversives who for years had terrorized Peru's mountain communities. As the bandits stormed out of their truck, brandishing automatic weapons, the Bensons thought this was it. After gruff questioning they were ordered into the terrorists' truck and driven off.

The missionaries were returning from a convention in a village where nearly three hundred had gathered to listen to the reading of the New Testament which the Bensons had just translated into the local Quecha dialect. Many had trusted Christ, and nineteen were baptized. The Quechas had sat on a hillside to watch several reels of movies based on the Gospel of Luke. A hush had fallen over the crowd as the images were projected onto a whitewashed adobe wall. Many had exclaimed, "It's Him! It's Jesus!" Several had wept, especially when Jesus was crucified. With the convention over, the Bensons had been on their way back to a reunion with their two little girls who were staying with friends. But instead, they were packed into a truck full of ruthless terrorists and guns.

In a situation that seemed so unreal, the missionaries sang hymn after hymn, and felt the enveloping love of God. Though repeatedly threatened, they were released at the end of the day. The bandits confiscated the missionaries' car and projection equipment. Helpless, but with faith and a silent prayer, Bruce offered them the color films of the life of Jesus.

A year later Jan Benson got a phone call, "One of the terrorists has become a Christian. He'd like to meet with you." Since her husband was away, a pastor went along. Face to face, twenty-three-year-old Jose, an experienced killer, told her how every time he killed brought him a thrill. Promoted to lead a battalion of 200 men, he himself was captured, imprisoned, and unexpectedly released. He met a pastor whom he had previously tried to kill, who then led him to Christ. Now he sat across from Jan.

"The day we captured you we intended to kill you. But each time we discussed it, something stopped us. After releasing you we returned to our camp in the jungle. Bored, some of our group decided to watch the films you had given us. One of our leaders said that Jesus was a revolutionary like us who wanted to change the bad He saw in society, but warned us against imperialistic rhetoric, and ordered us not to look at the films again. But that leader left camp next day, so we watched them over and over, hundreds of us. Many were so moved by Jesus' life and death that they wanted to lay down their arms and leave the movement." Jan felt goose-bumps rise on her flesh, as she now understood why God had permitted their capture a year before.[3]

If the picturing of Jesus' love and forgiveness on film could make such an impression, imagine the impact of the real-life drama on those actually present at the cross. The temporary suspension of judgment gave time for some to grasp the enormity of their crime, change their minds about Him, and ask and receive forgiveness. Minutes after Jesus' prayer, and for weeks thereafter, bystanders and contemporaries reassessed the import of that event. The reappraisal brought true faith to many. We have no complete tally of the conversions that took place in Jerusalem in the next few months as a result. The fruits of that wonderful prayer will never be fully known till the day the book of life is opened. But we do know of some individuals and groups who were impacted by Jesus' plea.

The first recorded change of heart belonged to one of the thieves. At first both thieves "heaped insults on him" (Mark 15:32). But no doom fell on them at that point. Then one of them began to do some thinking, even as his pal continued his mocking. Suddenly the repentant criminal spoke up, rebuking his companion-in-death, "Don't you fear God, since you are under the same sentence? We are punished justly, for we are getting what our deeds deserve. But this man has done nothing wrong." Then he turned to Jesus, "Remember me when you come into your kingdom." Somehow the repentant thief saw the sinfulness of his own life as opposed to the innocence of Jesus. Somehow he had sensed that Jesus was a king, would have a kingdom somewhere, and wanted Jesus to take him there. To which Jesus answered, "Today you will be with me in paradise" (Luke 23:39–43). The thief was pardoned. Jesus had the first answer to His prayer. If the other thief persisted in unbelief, he did not go out to join Jesus in paradise that day, but went out to wait the day of judgment.

What about the soldiers on duty at the crucifixion? Legend has enjoyed a field day speculating on the lives of those who drove the nails, creating many a fascinating story of conversion, now a part of church tradition. G. Campbell Morgan wrote, "We cannot depend upon legendary lore, except that we know that at the back of every legend there is some element of truth struggling to express itself; often failing to do it by overemphasis and grotesque emphases. I do not know, I have no evidence; but nothing would surprise me less when I reach the Land beyond, than to meet the man who drove the nails into the hands of Jesus, those who brought about His death."[4]

Whether or not any of the soldiers were converted then or later we do not know. But we do know that they, along with the centurion in charge of the military detail, were deeply moved. Matthew reports, "When the centurion and those with him who were guarding Jesus saw the earthquake and all that had happened, they were terrified, and exclaimed, 'Surely he was the Son of God.'"

Luke remarks that the centurion praised God and also said, "Surely this was a righteous man" (23:47). The centurion was pierced to the heart, and the soldiers with him, that he had supervised an act of injustice in crucifying an innocent man.

Some critics try to find a contradiction in the two statements, "He was the Son of God" and "He was a righteous man." However, could not the centurion have made both remarks since he was there over six hours, saw the darkness that lasted three hours, observed the magnanimous behavior of the victim on the middle cross, and had heard Him address God as His Father in two of His cries? It wasn't so strange for the centurion to call him

"Son of God" and "righteous man." While centurion and soldiers may not have fully grasped the significance of it all, the events may have prepared them to welcome later gospel preaching, perhaps even to join the ranks of the forgiven.

Luke records the strong effect of the crucifixion on the *crowd*, "When all the people who had gathered to witness this sight saw what took place, they beat their breasts and went away" (23:48). This was not the usual reaction to a public crucifixion. G. Campbell Morgan comments, "They had seen strange things that day. They had heard strange voices speak. The terror of darkness had certainly impressed them. They scattered, smiting on their breasts, with the sense of tragedy; may we not hope in the case of many of them, the sense of sin. As I read it, it would suggest a preparation for the day of Pentecost."[5]

At Pentecost, fifty days later, 3,000 acknowledged Jesus as Messiah and Lord, and received the forgiveness. Many of them had doubtless mocked Jesus as He hung on the cross. But since that day of infamy they had thought things over, perhaps visited the empty garden tomb, had come to realize what they had done, were cut to the heart by Peter's sermon, and repented. Another answer to Jesus' prayer; in fact 3,000 of them, and all on one day!

Even *priests* were affected by the events at Golgotha. Back in Jerusalem later that evening, they learned of another strange phenomenon. At the precise moment that Jesus expired, 3 p.m., the time of the evening sacrifice, fellow-priests on duty in the temple were shocked when the curtain to the Holy of Holies began to rip from top to bottom. Thoughtful priests knew that no human hand could barehandedly tear this thick veil in two. In their confusion they somehow mended the curtain. But as priests later ministered in the Holy Place and gazed on the patched veil, they asked themselves some questions. Was there some connection between Jesus' death and the temple curtain? Was that person on the cross by any chance the promised Passover Lamb of God? Did His death mean that no more animal sacrifices were required? And that the services of the priests were needed no more? And that's why the curtain was ripped—a sign that Jesus was the Messiah!

Some months after Pentecost the book of Acts gives this bit of news. "So the word of God spread. The number of disciples in Jerusalem increased rapidly, and a large number of priests became obedient to the faith" (6:7). Jesus' prayer was answered in a big way, for a large number of priests were added to the church.

We All Need Jesus' Spirit of Forgiveness

Paul wrote, "Bear with each other and forgive whatever grievances you may have against one another. Forgive as the Lord forgave you" (Col. 3:13). To keep this command we have both the example of Jesus and the power of the Holy Spirit, which we receive at the new birth to help us walk in newness of life.

Sitting by a river bank during rising tide, a man noticed a scorpion caught in the roots of a tree, and doomed to drown. Reaching down, the man tried to free the scorpion, but each time he did so, the scorpion struck at him. A bystander said, "Don't you know that's a scorpion, and it's the nature of a scorpion to sting?" To which the man replied, I know that, but it's my nature to save. Should I change my nature because the scorpion does not change its nature?"

It's the nature of evil people to strike unkindly to believers. And it should be the habit of believers to bless their enemies and to continue praying for them, even as their enemies continue their spiteful behavior. Do you have a neighbor who harasses you? Should you try to get back at him somehow? Or should try the approach of prayer, like Jesus on the cross.

Forgiveness is rare, always tough, but oh so lovely! The news section of *Christianity Today* says that with the lifting of many restrictions in Vietnam today most churches are alive and full. The reporter states that to sit in worship with 150 devout farmers and guitar-strumming youth in a small, evangelical church outside of Tam Ky in central Vietnam is to catch the vibrancy of God's Spirit. The aging pastor, Nguyen Xuan Vong, knows all about the hardship, war, and re-education. The concept of "enemy," is not academic for his members. Vong asks his people what is the Christian response to the enemy. Appealing to the example of Jesus on the cross, he answers, "You say to your enemies, 'Father, forgive them.'" [6]

Sometimes we can learn from animals. Sir Walter Scott had trouble accepting Jesus' advice to turn the other cheek. But the command took on new life when one day Scott threw a rock to chase away a stray dog. His aim was so good that he broke the dog's leg. Instead of running off, the dog limped over to him and licked his hand. Scott said that dog preached the meaning of the Sermon on the Mount as few ministers did, adding that he had not found people as ready to forgive their enemies as that animal.

Nothing makes us love a person as praying for him. If we feel resentment against someone and begin to pray for him, we'll find it hard to hold a grudge against that person whose name we have just lifted to God for His favor.

A meditation in *Our Daily Bread* told how during World War II Hitler ordered all religious groups to unite so as to bring them more easily under his control. Among the Brethren assemblies about half complied, and about half refused. Those who complied had a much easier time than those who didn't. Those who didn't faced harsh retaliation from the government. Almost every dissenting family lost a member in a concentration camp. When the war ended, bitter feelings ran deep between the two Brethren groups. Deciding that the tension had to be healed, leaders from both groups met together in a quiet retreat. For several days they merely spent time in private prayer, each person searching his own heart against the background of Christ's teachings. Then they came together. Francis Schaeffer, in relating this story, asked a friend who had been a participant, "What did you do then?" He replied that prayer for themselves and for each other brought them together, "We were just one." Confessing their hostility and bitterness, they yielded to the control of the Spirit who created an air of unity among them. Love, through prayer, dissolved their hatred. [7]

Stephen, the first church martyr, bruised, battered by rocks, and dying, fell to his knees and cried out a prayer like that of Jesus on the cross, "Lord, do not hold this sin against them" (Acts 7:60). Standing by was Saul of Tarsus, violent ringleader of early church persecution. Saul could never forgot Stephen's dying words which kept goading him until his conversion on the Damascus road. Saul later explained his violence against the church, "I acted in ignorance" (1 Tim. 1:13). Stephen's unrevengeful spirit contributed greatly to the sudden turnabout of persecutor Saul to preacher Paul. After his conversion, much of the New Testament centers on Paul. It could be said that Paul's travels and letters flowed from Stephen's forgiveness.

While a forgiving spirit can produce a powerful evangelistic impact, conversely failure to forgive can have a disastrous effect on the unforgiving person. The only clause in the Lord's Prayer singled out for attention dealt with forgiveness. Right after Jesus gave the Lord's Prayer, He commented, "For if you forgive men when they sin against you, your heavenly Father will also forgive you. But if you do not forgive men their sins, your Father will not forgive your sins" (Matt. 6:14–15).

When we continue to hold a grudge, it indicates that we have not grasped the enormity of our sin against God, and perhaps have not experienced the reality and joy of forgiven sins. An unforgiving spirit may signal an unforgiven spirit. Before his conversion a man was obsessed with vengeful thoughts toward a former friend who had shamefully abused him. But the day he came to the Lord with a broken and contrite heart, he thought only about his own sins—the thought of how he had been wronged took a dim spot in the back of his mind. When someone remarked to him that he no longer spoke of his injustice, he responded with tears, "Oh, it's such a little thing. I've been forgiven so much!"

If God incarnate could forgive puny, wicked men for the greatest felony in history—crucifying the Lord of Glory, then no manmade excuse could ever justify failure to forgive a fellow-creature for whatever far lesser crime.

An unforgiving spirit hinders our prayer life. To nurse a grudge blocks the ear of God. Jesus warned, "And when you stand praying, if you hold anything against anyone, forgive him, so that your Father in heaven may forgive you your sins" (Mark 11:25). An unforgiving spirit may inhibit other aspects of worship. Jesus said, "If you are offering your gift at the altar and there remember that your brother has something against you, leave your gift there in front of the altar. First go and be reconciled to your brother; then come and offer your gift" (Matt. 5:23–24).

Miriam Payne Lemcio relates an eloquent incident in her biography of her father, long-time Houghton College president. Her teenage sister, Margie, stricken with polio which later proved fatal, was hospitalized in Buffalo, N.Y. Her father went to the hospital every chance he could, as college duties permitted. About two months after her admission Margie's mother called from the hospital as he was finishing his work. Normally his wife would be heading home at this time, but today felt she shouldn't leave Margie alone. Margie, weak and discouraged, had asked, "Pray hard for me tonight, Mother." Payne borrowed a friend's pickup truck and headed the 60 miles to Buffalo. Writes Miriam, "As he drove, he felt the Lord speaking to him about a bitterness of spirit he had felt toward a certain staff member who had been very critical of him. Dad stopped the truck, went to a pay phone and called the man, asking his forgiveness. He didn't want anything to impede or diminish his prayers in behalf of his daughter. . . . It's a fairly remarkable matter that a man in a supreme crisis of life, analyzing himself most critically in the sure knowledge that he cannot concentrate on intercession for his daughter, that that man comes up with ONE name only!"[8]

When Leonardo da Vinci was working on his painting *The Last Supper*, he became angry with a man, lost his temper, and lashed out bitterly at him. Back at his canvas he attempted to continue his work on the face of Jesus but was so upset that he couldn't compose himself for the delicate task. Finally he put down his brush, sought out the man, and asked his forgiveness. With apology accepted the artist was able to return to his workshop and finish painting the face of Jesus. It's hard for an unforgiving person to truly reflect the love of Jesus. But when we do model His forgiving spirit, we make a powerful statement to those who, in rejecting Jesus, do not know what they are doing.

Notes
1. A. T. Robertson, *Translation of Luke's Gospel* (New York: G.H. Doran, 1924).
2. Helen Barret Montgomery, *Centenary Translation of the New Testament* (Chicago: American Baptist Publications, 1984).
3. Jan Benson with Kathryn Moore, "By Life or By Death" in *In Other Words,* December 1991.
4. *The Gospel According to Luke,* p. 270.
5. *Ibid.,* p. 274.
6. *Christianity Today,* 22 November 1993, p. 44.
7. *Our Daily Bread,* 4 October 1992.
8. Lemcio, Miriam Payne, *Deo Volente* (Houghton, N.Y.: Houghton College, 1987), p. 156.

CHAPTER 11

Facing Death Confidently

Sir Walter Raleigh, British soldier, explorer, adventurer, founder of the colony of Virginia, and favorite of Queen Elizabeth I, fell out of favor during the reign of James I, and was brought to the executioner's block. He took off his hat and coat so nonchalantly that witnesses said he seemed as free from fear as if he had come there as a spectator instead of as a victim. He insisted on handling the ax, and feeling its sharp edge, remarked to the executioner, "This is sharp medicine, but it is a physician for all diseases." Then, asked which way he preferred to lay his head on the block, he replied, "So long as the heart is right, it is no matter which way the head lies."

Shakespeare wrote,

> The tongues of dying men
> Enforce attention like deep harmony;
> Where words are scarce, they're seldom spent in vain,
> For they breathe truth that breathe their words in pain.

The final words which fell from the lips of the Lord Jesus at the end of the crucifixion were most significant. No longer feeling forsaken by His heavenly Father, with the deepest of the agony past, and His mission accomplished, He confidently surrendered Himself in death, saying, "Father, into your hands I commit my spirit," then breathed His last (Luke 23:46).

Because of His triumphant departure, multitudes of His followers through the centuries have been able to face death boldly. Polycarp, Bishop of Smyrna and disciple of the apostle John, just before martyrdom by fire, refused to recant his faith. Instead he made this affirmation of devotion: "Eighty and six years have I now served Christ, and He has never done me the least wrong; how, then, can I blaspheme my King and my Savior?"

Before the lions reached him in the arena at Rome, Ignatius, Bishop of Antioch and second-century martyr, said, "I am the wheat of Christ; I am going to be ground with the teeth of wild beasts, that I may be found pure bread."

James Usher (1581–1656), known for his chronology of the Bible, died with the publican's prayer on his lips, "O, Lord, forgive me, especially my sins of omission. 'God be merciful to me, a sinner!'"

Adoniram Judson (1788–1850), pioneer missionary to Burma, died at sea. Before he breathed his last and his body was committed to the deep, he said to those around him, "I go with the gladness of a boy bounding away from school. I feel so strong in Christ."

Among frequently quoted last words are those of D. L. Moody (1837–1899) who joyfully exclaimed in his final moments, "I see earth receding; heaven is opening. God is calling me, and I must go. This is my coronation day. It is glorious."

Understandably many on their deathbed have used words similar to those of Jesus. The first Christian martyr, Stephen, prayed as they stoned him, "Lord Jesus, receive my spirit" (Acts 7:59). Jesus' dying prayer teaches many lessons.

Jesus Faced Death

As the consciousness of His mission began to dawn more clearly, Jesus came to realize that He had come to earth to offer up His body as a sacrifice for mankind's sin. Though He was born to die, we were born to live. At our birth doctors and relatives happily announced that a new life had entered the world. But though born to live, we too will die. Just as Jesus uttered last words, so we too some day will speak our final statement.

Die we will. To our first parents God warned that disobedience to His command would bring death. When our first parents ate the forbidden fruit, they died spiritually with physical death following years later. The sentence of death has been passed on to every member of the human race, only Enoch and Elijah escaping when caught up by God into heaven. Death has a key to every home on every street, and to the remotest hut on the farthest island. Death cares not for our plans. A lady may begin a letter and never sign it. A man may start a journey and never complete it. Sometimes the young die before the old and the strong before the weak. Every tombstone is death's pulpit, and every newspaper carries his advertisement.

In early centuries the noblemen of China kept their coffins ready-made in their chambers as a reminder of the imminence of death. The Egyptians at their lavish banquets made it a practice to place a dead man's skull in a prominent corner as a restraint to their pleasures. Neither can today's elite escape the grim reaper. Before his death in 1990 Malcolm Forbes, reputedly the world's wealthiest person, co-authored a best-selling book, *They Went That-a-Way*, about the unusual final hours of 175 of this planet's most famous people. A Connecticut hearse bore this license plate, U-2.

How silently the years sneak up on us. A gray hair here, another there, till hardly aware of their arrival, we find our head covered with gray hair—or none. Before long, and oh, so gradually, eyes dim, legs wobble, teeth decay, ears dull, mind forgets, and strength wanes.

Someone listed the five B's of aging: bunions, bifocals, baldness, bridges, and bulges. A person's history can be summed up in terms of three tablets: school tablet, aspirin tablet, and stone tablet. The Bible speaks of life as a tale that is told, a flower that fades, grass that withers, a shadow that declines, and vapor that vanishes.

On the left side of his desk a business man kept a picture of the hospital where he was born. On the right side was a picture of the local cemetery featuring a monument with his family name carved thereon. In between sat a picture of himself. The pictures seemed to say, "Don't forget, these are where you checked in, and where you'll check out." Die we will.

A mother was seriously ill. Her little girl overheard the doctor tell her daddy, "I'm afraid your wife will be leaving this earth when the leaves begin to fall." The child loved her mother dearly, and looking out the window one late September day, knew the time was short. Feverishly she ran outside to every tree she could find on their spacious lawn. Night fell. Not seeing her in the house, her daddy became alarmed. He found her under a tree and asked why she was crying. The little girl sobbed out, "I heard the doctor say that mommy would go away from this earth when the leaves begin to fall. And I've been hurrying as fast as I could all day, tying all the leaves to the branches. I love mommy so much. I don't want the leaves to fall." But the leaves will fall for all of us some day.

Jesus Faced Death Voluntarily

Unless, unwisely, we take our own life, we have no say as to the time of our death. We cannot determine the day nor the hour of our demise. But Jesus died at the very second He chose. The early church stressed this truth. Augustine said, "He gave up His life because He willed it, when He willed it, and as He willed it." Whatever physical cause medicine may assign to His death, He expired of His own volition.

Many plots were made against Jesus' life, but all failed because He had the keys of death and would not let anyone take His life before His hour had come—the hour at which He had chosen to die. The list of attempts on His life is imposing:

- Herod's slaughter of infant boys in the Bethlehem area (Matt. 2:16–18).
- Was the presence of wild beasts during the wilderness temptation a Satanic effort to destroy Him? (Mark 1:13).
- The devil's suggestion to jump off the temple pinnacle (Matt. 4:5–6).
- His hometown people pushing Him to the brow of the hill outside Nazareth to throw Him over the cliff (Luke 4:28–30).
- After Jesus healed the invalid at the pool of Bethesda and called God His own Father, the leaders "tried all the harder to kill Him" (John 5:18).
- After Jesus healed the man with the withered hand in the synagogue, the Pharisees "went out and began to plot with the Herodians how they might kill Jesus" (Mark 3:6).

- Was the violent storm on Galilee a satanic attempt to drown Him? (Mark 4:35–41).
- At the Feast of Tabernacles in Jerusalem it was known by both Jesus and the people that a plot was under foot to kill Him (John 7:19, 25). Though they tried to seize Him, no one laid a hand on Him, and the temple guard, sent to apprehend Him, returned empty-handed because "No one ever spoke the way this man does" (vv. 30, 45–46). His hour to die had not yet come.
- After a dialogue in which Jesus declared, "Before Abraham was born, I am," the Pharisees "picked up stones to stone him, but Jesus hid himself, slipping away from the temple grounds" (John 8:58–59).
- At the Feast of Dedication, where Jesus claimed to be one with the Father and thus equal with God His enemies "picked up stones to stone him" (John 10:30–32). This continuing threat was why Jesus was out of the area when Lazarus died (11:7–8).
- Herod had plans to finish Jesus off. One day the Pharisees came to Him and warned, "Leave this place and go somewhere else. Herod wants to kill you" (Luke 13:31).
- The Sanhedrin plot to take His life was backed up by high priest Caiaphas' prophecy about the expediency of one man dying to save the nation (John 11:45–51).
- After Jesus uttered the parable of the wicked farmers who killed the owner's son, the scribes and chief priests "looked for a way to arrest him immediately, because they knew he had spoken this parable against them" (Luke 20:19).
- Finally their plot began to materialize. At first, when the leaders were looking for some sly way to arrest Him, they said not during the feast lest the people riot (Mark 14:1–2). But with the help of Judas' betrayal they decided not to wait till after the feast. Unwittingly they were fitting into Jesus' predetermined plan to die at the time of the offering of the Passover lamb that Good Friday afternoon. John says, "It was just before the Passover Feast. Jesus knew that the time had come for him to leave this world and go to the Father" (13:1).

At death, as strength ebbs, the human voice grows weaker. But Doctor Luke records that Jesus cried His final words with a loud voice (Luke 23:46). Jesus did not surrender to death in weakness, but in strength beckoned death to serve Him.

A dying person, especially in a partially reclining position, often tries to raise his head in the closing moments, a last effort to replenish the lungs with life-giving oxygen. Then as life ebbs, the head falls forward on the chest. But in Jesus' case He bowed His head before He died, a strong suggestion that He purposefully offered up His life.

Jesus said, "I lay down my life for the sheep. . . . No one takes it from me, but I lay it down of my own accord. I have authority to lay it down" (John 10:11–18). When the soldiers came to break the legs of the victims to hurry their deaths, they were surprised to find Jesus already expired. He had dismissed His spirit voluntarily at the precise moment He willed, a power beyond the jurisdiction of mortals.

Jesus faced death victoriously. The conversation at a party suddenly hushed when someone remarked that a friend had just learned from his doctor that he had cancer. A bystander, a prominent psychiatrist, handsome and in the pink of health, admitted, "I'm scared to death of dying." Smiling sheepishly at his frail pun, he nevertheless expressed honestly what so many folks feel.

Jesus knew life existed beyond the grave. Job's age-old question asks, "If a man dies, will he live again?" Jesus' final cry answers triumphantly, "There is life beyond the grave. Father, I'm leaving here to be with you." In Jesus' case He was not going to a place where He had not been before. He had come to earth from heaven. Less than a day before His death, He said to His disciples, "I came from the Father and entered the world; now I am leaving the world and going back to the Father" (John 16:28).

Schilder in his classic *Christ Crucified* says, "For now that Christ has completely finished the course of obedience by permitting His body also to be broken, now Paradise must receive Him in His glory. . . . Therefore the angel who guards the gate of Paradise must stand aside when He impressively approaches . . . he says to himself that this man must enter."[1] Jesus had promised the repentant thief that they would be together in Paradise that very day (Luke 23:43).

Schilder also states that between death and the resurrection Jesus was "still in the intermediary condition, the condition of the 'unclothed soul' who is in Paradise without his body."[2] Jesus' spirit waited those three days till Easter morn to rejoin His resurrected body. Then after forty days on earth during which He showed Himself alive to His disciples and taught them, He then triumphantly ascended into heaven, both spirit and body, to sit down at the right hand of the Majesty on high. Some believe that sometime during that intermediate period between His death and Sunday He descended into Hades and preached unto the spirits in prison (1 Peter 3:18–20). Schilder titles the two chapters that deal with Jesus' final cry, "Christ Goes Out; God Goes On" and "Christ Passing Out And On." This prayer confirms the truth of life beyond the grave.

Jesus' prayer is a quote from Psalm 31:5. Interestingly when the psalmist commits his spirit into the hands of the Lord, he is not thinking of death but is asking the Lord to prolong his life by protecting him from the trap of his enemies. He commits himself into God's hand, convinced that his life will overcome the dangers and be prolonged for further service for God. Jesus adopts this prayer at His demise as affirmation of the uninterrupted flow of life; despite death His spirit will live on in the presence of His Father.

Jesus had utmost confidence in His Father in the hour of death. A few minutes earlier Jesus' fourth cry from the cross formed a question which indicated a struggle and a sense of abandonment: "My God, my God, why hast thou forsaken me?" Now the word *Father* implied an answer to His prayer for help in His desolation. The Father has made Himself known to the Son again. Jesus has regained full serenity by the recovery of His Father's face and fellowship. No safer place could He seek a refuge for His departing spirit than "*into Your hands.*" The hand of God is a figure of strength and security and its plural—both hands.

"*I commit*" has the idea of entrusting to, or setting before, or making a deposit of a task (Luke 12:48), or of a person (Acts 14:23), or of content of preaching (2 Tim. 2:2). On the cross Jesus placed His spirit into the care of His heavenly Father.

This is why Paul could write similar words from prison near the end of His life, "I know whom I have believed, and am convinced that he is able to guard what I have entrusted to him for that day" (2 Tim. 1:12).

On earth Jesus suffered most of the vicissitudes that can befall the human race. He knew what it was to be hungry, tired, thirsty, insulted, despised, betrayed, suffer pain, and to stand by the grave of a loved one. He also knew what it was to die. His dying prayer was so simple that anyone who believes in Him can repeat it after Him. Many have echoed His identical words such as Augustine, Luther, Bernard, Knox, Basil, and Felix Manz. John Huss, on the way to be burned at the stake while his enemies were gleefully taunting him by giving his soul over to the devil, said with sure, calm faith, "But I commit my spirit into Thy hands, O Lord Jesus Christ, who has redeemed it."

Because Jesus died victoriously, we know that death does not end it all, but rather ushers believers into the Father's presence. Perhaps no other place shows us more graphically the ability of Christians to face death courageously than the catacombs near Rome, a vast labyrinth of subterranean galleries where in times of persecution early believers hid, worshiped, and buried their dead. Not used after the fourth century and overgrown with vegetation, the catacombs were forgotten till their discovery in the sixteenth century. Excavations revealed some fifty catacombs with three hundred miles of long, narrow corridors, usually about eight feet high and five feet wide, containing on both sides rows of long, low horizontal recesses, closed by a marble slab or painted tiles. Galleries were found at several levels, one above the other, ventilated by vertical shafts running up to the outside.

I spent a delightful two hours down in the catacombs of St. Sebastian and St. Domilla, impressed by the different symbols and inscriptions scratched by relatives or friends—a name, a prayer, words of hope and faith, or a biblical scene showing belief in immortality. Frequently depicted was the raising of Lazarus, the Jonah story, the Noah episode, the Hebrews in the fiery furnace, and Daniel in the lions' den, all of which portray triumph over death. Both pagans and Christians buried their dead in the catacombs, but what a difference in epitaphs.

Pagan inscriptions read like this:

"Live for the present hour since we are sure of nothing else."
"I will lift my hands against the gods who took me away at the the age of twenty, though I had done no harm."

"Once I was not. Now I am not. I know nothing about it, and it is no concern of mine."
"Traveler, curse me not as you pass, for I am in darkness and cannot answer."

When Christian graves were opened, skeletons revealed heads severed from body, ribs broken, bones calcined. Simple epitaphs vividly contrasted with heathen sentiments:

"Here lies Marcia, put to rest in a dream of peace."
"Lawrence to his sweetest son, borne away of angels."
"Called away, he went in peace."
"Victorious in peace and in Christ."

We die as we live. Some unbelievers do manage to muster a seemingly courageous gallows humor. Oscar Wilde, Irish dramatist and wit, dying in a cheap rooming house, and flip to the end, remarked, "It's the wallpaper or me—one of us has to go."

Unbelievers most often remain in unbelief, though the bold front displayed in prosperity collapses during declining health. A man who spent months in a jail that housed prisoners with not long to live reported that no atheist died quietly. Time after time he saw men enter as hardened unbelievers, only to lose their atheistic bravado in the face of death, but still dying as unbelievers.

For years a business man devoted much of his spare time and money to prove that God did not exist. Irrevocably he held there was no afterlife, neither heaven nor hell. Decades later an old friend saw him at a convention but hardly recognized him. It was evident that he had lost his poise, and acted like a man awaiting a death sentence. At seventy-one, he learned that he had less than a year to live. He told how during hospital treatment he had met a lady facing her end with a smiling face. Conscripted to witness her deathbed will, he had heard her joyfully exclaim, "Now I am ready to leave this painracked body to meet my Maker, my husband, my father, my mother, and all my friends who have gone before me. Won't that be wonderful!" Said the atheist in a hoarse voice with tears starting down his pale, wrinkled cheeks, "Look at me. I've lain awake many nights since I learned my days were numbered, staring at the ceiling with nothing to look forward to except that my life would end in a handful of ashes. That's the difference between me, an atheist, and the lady I have described. She, believing, faces her final days with a smile. Here am I, a nonbeliever, with every moment a nightmare, facing nothing but a cold tomb." He hesitated, then added, "I would shove my hands into a bed of red hot coals if by so doing I could secure a belief in a Supreme Being and an afterlife."

Jesus lived a life of prayer, and He died with a prayer on His lips. Jesus' life was saturated with prayer. The Gospels record two dozen occasions when He actually engaged in the practice of prayer. As we have seen in earlier chapters, He prayed regularly, and at every milestone and crisis.

Just as mothers today teach their children to repeat at bedtime, "Now I lay me down to sleep; I pray the Lord my soul to keep," so Jewish mothers then taught their little ones to say the prayer of Psalm 31:5, "Lord, into Thy hands I commit my spirit." The evening prayer of little children became the dying prayer of the Savior. Perhaps He had prayed it often Himself at the evening hour. Now, how appropriate for Him, with enemies defeated, to calmly pray the children's evening prayer and fall asleep in the Father's hand in the most blessed repose of all.

Countless saints through the centuries have died with a prayer on their lips. David Livingstone, pioneer missionary to Africa, died on his knees deep in the interior of that continent.

Jesus' life was saturated with Scripture, and He died with Scripture on His lips. Jesus used Scripture to defeat Satan when tempted. Every time Satan tried to entice Him, Jesus answered with a quote from Deuteronomy. Often in discussion with the scribes and Pharisees, Jesus said, "It is written," or "Have ye not read?" When it came to die, Jesus' last word was a quote from Psalm 31:5. His fourth cry was a quote from the Psalm 22:1.

As Martin Luther neared death, he repeated Jesus' dying prayer three times. As he breathed his last, he quoted John 3:16 and Psalm 68:20 which speaks of escaping death through the Lord.

F. B. Meyer, well-known English preacher, dismissed the enemy of death with confidence. His last articulate words were, "Read me something from the Bible, something brave and triumphant."

Before he died, Robert Bruce, prominent Edinburgh preacher,

called for the family Bible and said to his daughter, "Cast up to me the eighth chapter of Romans, and set my finger on these words, 'I am persuaded that neither death nor life . . . shall be able to separate me from the love of God which is in Christ Jesus my Lord.'" Then he asked, "Is my finger on them?" Assured, he said, "Now God be with you my children; I have just breakfasted with you, and shall sup with my Lord Jesus this night."

Jesus lived a life filled with deep, inner joy, and He died with poise and peace. Jesus' ministry was characterized by composure. He was never in a hurry, never flustered, always self-assured and calm of spirit. Someone referred to His pace as the "gait of Galilee." On the eve of His crucifixion He spoke of "My peace." And He died with profound serenity, no agitation, alarm, or anxiety.

Jesus' example should give courage to believers to confront the king of terrors and to see death as a vanquished foe whose sting has been removed. When the flesh fails, the spirit will be in good hands. When Susanna Wesley lay dying, her last request just before she lost her speech was, "Children, as soon as I am released, sing a song of praise to God." Soon as she passed away, loved ones gathered round the bed and sang a hymn. Her son John Wesley said of early Methodists, "Our people die well."

For Catherine Booth, cofounder of the Salvation Army, it was all upbeat. "The waters are rising, but so am I. I am not going under but over. Do not be concerned about dying; go on living well, and dying will be right."

The hope exemplified in Jesus' prayer brought a new attitude toward death. Martyrs faced death with heroic cheerfulness. Believers possessed a tranquil assurance. Like Paul, they knew that to be absent from the body meant to be present with the Lord. As a pastor, I have had several parishioners give me an advance outline of their funeral service, including the hymns they wanted sung, clearly reflecting a celebration of triumph.

Jesus Faced Death Vicariously

The word "commit" means to deposit for safekeeping. Having paid the price for our salvation, Jesus was ready to lay down His life. In trust and triumph He was depositing His soul into the safekeeping of His Father. But when He deposited His soul into the Father's hand, He also committed to His Father for safe-keeping all those who believe in the Son. There nothing, not even death, can separate us from God's love. Jesus had already suffered in our place all the crushing blows of God's wrath against our iniquities and was about to appear in heaven as our High Priest to deposit Himself as an offering in our behalf. When Jesus deposited His soul with God, he did it for us.

Hebrews emphasized the superiority of Jesus over Old Testament priests who needed to offer up sacrifices for their own sins as well as for those of the people. And they had to do it repeatedly. But Jesus was "holy, blameless, pure. . . . Unlike the other high priests, he" did "not need to offer sacrifices day after day, first for his own sins, and then for the sins of the people. He sacrificed for their sins once for all when he offered himself" (7:26–27). Then He took His sacrifice to heaven, and sat down at the right hand of God (10:12). He did not enter a manmade sanctuary, but "He entered heaven itself, now to appear for us in God's presence" (9:24).

When Jesus finished His once-for-all sacrifice, He deposited it with the Father as a guarantee of our acceptance with Him. So when our turn comes to die, we'll be able to die like Jesus, and follow Him through death into the Father's presence forever. Because of Jesus' finished work on the cross, we'll be able to say, "Father, I deposit my spirit with You. I'm coming home."

I shall never forget the events connected with the homegoing of David Goodwin who, as pastor of a small Canadian church, had started me teaching my first Sunday school class at the age of sixteen. Later he pastored a church in Moline, Illinois. We kept in touch through the years, especially during the period his daughter, an internationally known harpist, studied at Juilliard School of Music and lived near us in the New York City area.

Then I learned in late 1969 that Dave had become ill and that his daughter had gone home to take care of him. When spring came without further word, I phoned his home in East Moline to find out how he was doing. His daughter answered, quietly informing me that her father had slowly declined in health, that his weight had gone from 180 to 90 pounds, that he was confined to bed most of the time, getting out only Sundays to deliver a sermon, that they would wheel him into the sanctuary just before sermon time, that with his suit hanging on his skin and bones and with a little table and mike he would faintly but bravely preach from his wheelchair, and that that very afternoon he had performed two weddings from his wheelchair. Then his daughter asked this stabbing question, "My father knows he has cancer and is going to die. And he wants you to come and preach his funeral sermon. Will you be able to do it? Keep me posted on your summer plans."

Then she connected me with her father in his bedroom. In soft voice he told me that he was going to leave this world soon. Three Sundays later, in California for our denomination's annual convention, word reached me that Dave had passed away that afternoon. His daughter told me that morning upon awakening he had said, "This is the day. I'm going home today." Then he had asked her to read his two favorite Psalms, the 103rd and 91st. Then he quoted the 23rd Psalm, including the verse, "Even though I walk through the valley of the shadow of death, I will fear no evil, for you are with me." Moments later he died.

Switching my plane flight, I arrived in East Moline in time for the viewing. Over 1200 came to pay respects. Dave had pastored the church for thirty-four years, and was deeply loved in the community, also serving as chaplain of the state hospital.

I learned that on his final Sundays he preached from 2 Peter chapter 1. "So I will always remind you of these things, even though you know them and are firmly established in the truth you now have. I think it is right to refresh your memory as long as I live in the tent of this body, because I know that I will soon put it aside, as our Lord Jesus Christ has made clear to me. And I will make very effort to see that after my departure you will always be able to remember these things" (12–15).

Hundreds attended the overflow service. It was my privilege to give the sermon, but the most moving part of the program was the harp music, skillfully played by his daughter. From her instrument, positioned beside the casket, came the beautiful strains of two hymns he had requested, "I heard the voice of Jesus say, 'Come unto Me and rest,'" and "Safe in the arms of Jesus." That's where Dave was—safe in the presence of Jesus.

Members of his congregation commented, "For thirty-four years Pastor Dave has taught us how to live. Now in these last few months, he has taught us how to die."

Notes
1. Schilder, *Christ Crucified* (Grand Rapids: Wm. B. Eerdmans, 1944), p. 499.
2. Ibid., p. 500.

CHAPTER 12

Succeeding in Prayer— Jesus' Principles

Among my 1992 Christmas letters was one titled, "Five Somewhere Among Five Million," written by John Barcus, a longtime missionary-friend who served under the Gospel Missionary Union in North Africa. Semi-retired and a widower, Barcus had joined a Middle East tour the previous October, stayed on two weeks in Bethlehem, then spent the next four weeks working as a volunteer in a modern 1400-bed hospital near Tel Aviv. His main assignment was to deliver and collect food trays twice a day.

His chief purpose in going to Israel was to find five men in their sixties whom he had discipled nearly forty years earlier in Morocco. All five had emigrated to Israel. Barcus knew their names but had no idea where to find them among five million other Israelites. Perhaps they had changed their names. Said Barcus, "No government agency in Israel could give me any help, but heaven could. I prayed and wondered how contact might be restored. The Lord answered in marvelous links."

Walking down Jaffa Street in Jerusalem, Barcus passed a shop with a sign "Bible Society" in English. "Maybe someone here can help me," he thought. The manager quickly became interested in the quest and made a few phone calls, but to no avail. He suggested Barcus contact a Victor Smadja who came from Morocco and might have known these Jewish men and possibly their whereabouts. As it turned out, Smadja, a Christian, had never been in Morocco. He had been born in Tunisia, then came to Israel and set up a prosperous business. On the side he printed Bibles and New Testaments which he gave away in response to newspaper ads.

The first name on Barcus' list of "missing persons" was Eliyahu Maman. "There are a lot of Maman families in Israel," commented Smadja, "and Eliyahu is a popular name." Smadja later confided that he questioned Barcus' sanity in hoping to find any of them after so long. But generous, he had his secretary write dozens of letters to try to ferret out one of the men. No success.

But one day he showed Barcus a letter from a teenage army lass, thanking Smadja for a book he had sent her dealing with the Messiah. She said her father agreed with the book. Her family name was Maman, the address down in the Negev desert. "I'd like to meet her father," said Smadja. "Do you suppose he could be your Eliyahu Maman?" A phone call revealed that he was an immigrant from Morocco, was indeed Eliyahu Maman, was thrilled to hear that Barcus was in Israel, and wanted to see him soon.

Said Barcus, "What a reunion we had!" Maman was still firm in his faith, even though without Christian fellowship at all for thirty years. To top it off, he had the phone numbers of two of the other five Barcus was seeking. And they lived not far from the hospital where Barcus was working. Again, what reunions!

One pulled out a picture which Barcus had taken of him and his wife on their wedding day thrity years before. The other said, "Monsieur Barcus, when I came here I dreamed for twenty years that someday you would come to visit me in Israel. Then I stopped dreaming, but here you are!" He had changed his name from the one Barcus remembered. Said Barcus, "I would never have found him without God's wonderful leading in answer to prayer!" And what a thrill for Barcus to find these men with the embers of truth, lit thirty years earlier, still burning in their hearts. Friends in Israel continue to look for the other two.

Jesus had continual success in prayer. By the grave of Lazarus He prayed, "I thank you that you have heard me. I knew that you always hear me" (John 11:41–42). Jesus made prayer a top priority in His ministry, and His prayers were answered. In this final chapter we'll review, rephrase, and augment some of the principles that made His praying eminently effective.

Jesus Based His Praying on a Right Relationship with His Father

Of the twenty-three occasions Jesus prayed, eight are direct quotes. Seven of those eight directly quoted prayers begin with Jesus addressing God as "Father." The listing of those seven prayers should highlight His repeated use of "Father." And a logical explanation can be suggested for the one omitting "Father."

"I praise you, Father, Lord of heaven and earth, because you had hidden these things from the wise and learned, and revealed them to little children. Yes, Father, for this was your good pleasure" (Luke 10:21). "Father" is used twice.

"Father, I thank you that you have heard me. I knew that you always hear me, but I said this for the benefit of the people standing here, that they may believe that you sent me" (John 11:41–42).

"'Father, save me from this hour'? No, it was for this very reason I came to this hour. Father, glorify your name!" (John 12:27–28). "Father" is used twice.

From His High Priestly Prayer: "Father, the time has come. Glorify your Son, that your Son may glorify you" (17:1). "And now, Father, glorify me in your presence with the glory I had with you before the world began" (v. 5). "Holy Father, protect them by the power of your name. . . ." (v. 11). "I pray also for those who will believe in me through their message, that all of them may be one, Father, just as you are in me and I am in you" (vv. 20–21). "Father, I want those you have given me to be with me where I am, and to see my glory. . . . (v. 24). "Righteous Father, though the world does not know you, I know you, and they know that you have sent me" (v. 25). "Father" occurs six times.

"My Father, if it is possible, may this cup be taken from me. Yet not as I will, but as you will" (Matt. 26:39). "My Father, if it is not possible for this cup to be taken away unless I drink it, may your will be done" (v. 42). He prayed the same the third time, using "Father" three times in Gethsemane.

"Father, forgive them, for they know do not what they are doing" (Luke 23:34).

"Father, into your hands I commit my spirit" (Luke 23:46).

In these seven prayers Jesus addressed God as "Father" a total of sixteen times. The only quoted prayer which He did not begin by saying "Father" was His fourth word from the cross, "My God, my God, why have you forsaken me?" (Matt. 27:46; Mark 15:34). The omission of "Father" here has a reasonable explanation. This was the climactic moment of Jesus' crucifixion sufferings. It had been dark for three hours. In silence Jesus had borne the penalty for our sins, endured the wrath of hell, and for a little while sensed that a holy God had turned His back. Feeling forsaken by his Father, He cried out, "God," instead of "Father."

Jesus based His praying on His close relationship with the Father. Similarly, if we would prevail in prayer, we must enter the Lord's presence as His children. Though not sons of God in the unique relationship possessed by Jesus, yet when we trust Jesus as our Savior, we are born again into the family of God and become His children (John 1:12). The fatherhood of God is a new emphasis revealed in the Gospels. As God's children, we receive the spirit of adoption, are enabled to cry "Father" or "Abba" which could be translated "Daddy" (Rom. 8:15), and have the right to boldly enter our "Daddy's" presence and make known our requests. The Father hears the prayers of His own children.

Does God ever answer the prayers of unbelievers? In His common grace He seems to sometimes grant their petitions. But His sons and daughters have prior claim. Jesus taught His followers to enter the place of prayer by saying, "Our Father."

Jesus Prayed at Regular Times and in Quiet Places

Regular times. Regular synagogue attendance was a habit of Jesus (Luke 4:16), doubtless taught Him by His parents, who also would have instilled in Him the custom of praying three times daily. We are given one instance of His praying early in the morning (Mark 1:35). We know of several times He prayed in the evening, e.g., Matt. 14:23. When He retreated to desert or mountain to pray (Luke 5:16), it could have been the hour of prayer. During His final week Jesus went out *as usual* to the Mount of Olives (Luke 22:39), where we know He prayed and often spent the night (Luke 21:37), rising ready for morning prayer.

Some folks claim they are always in the spirit of prayer, so need not schedule any regular time. Though Jesus never specified any particular hour, nor how often we should pray each day, He evidently observed fixed times. To pray today Jesus' way would require us to find time somewhere in our daily routine for personal devotions, then discipline ourselves to keep it, whether morning or night.

Missionary J. Hudson Taylor said, "Satan will always find you something to do when you ought to be occupied about prayer and Bible study, if it is only arranging a window blind."[1]

Ken Taylor, publisher of *The Living Bible*, wrote, "After many years of ups and downs in my devotional life—of success mingled with failure—I realize there is no solution except to make a regular appointment with God and to stick to it . . . I must ask God to help me stay on a regular schedule. When I don't, I know I have missed the greatest privilege and opportunity of that day. My own time with God is usually before breakfast, although I sometimes keep my appointment late at night or even during the night."[2]

Quiet Place. It's possible to pray anywhere, even in the sauna, in busy traffic waiting for the light to change, in crowded doctor's offices, or amid the swaying seats of commuter trains. But although it's wise to take advantage of free moments in unlikely places, to be like Jesus we should take time to withdraw from the crowded places to search out some quiet spot. He prayed in gardens and deserts and on mountaintops. He had his favorite hideouts. One wonders if in the sweltering heat of the rugged wilderness He might have sought the coolness of a cave. To escape the pressure of the multitude Jesus worked hard to find quiet. He urged His followers to enter a closet to pray, not that a closet has some special holiness; rather, it provides solitude. The place where you find calm becomes your closet.

In 1963 when Ken Taylor began to publish *Living Letters*, he had to decide if he should leave his job as Director of Moody Press to devote more time to paraphrasing more of the Bible.

Could he make it without his salary? What if *Living Letters* flopped? At lunchtime he would climb to one of the empty floors of Moody's oldest building and, pacing back and forth, pray for wisdom. Other times he would slip down into the subbasement of Moody Press to a window well that became his prayer closet. [2]

Edith Schaeffer tells in *The Life of Prayer* of sitting outside Denver airport and seeing a janitor on the other end of the bench. Beside him was a large cart, full of brooms, mops, a pail, thick clothes, and cleaning fluid. She learned that he was on his lunch break. Here he had a quiet time of prayer each noon, saying "It's too noisy in there." [3]

In one part of Africa early converts chose their own individual place outside the village where they went for prayer. Each made a private footpath through the brush to reach his "prayer room." Grass overgrowing a path betrayed declining prayer in that person's life. Out of concern for each other's spiritual welfare anyone noticing an overgrown prayer path would lovingly warn, "Brother, there's grass on your path!"

Jesus Didn't Limit Himself to Rigid Prayer Patterns

To pray today Jesus' way permits latitude and variety.

Not circumscribed by a prepared text. At times Jesus prayed in logically outlined petitions as He did in the High Priestly Prayer and the Lord's Prayer. The former progresses in an orderly fashion from prayer for Himself, for the apostles, then for future believers. The latter begins with God's name, kingdom, and will, then turns to man's need for bread, forgiveness, and protection from evil.

Prepared, written prayers have their advantages both in private but especially in public worship. But Jesus also prayed in a free, seemingly unpremeditated outflow of emotion, as at Lazarus' grave, in Gethsemane, and on the cross. Similarly, we can pour out our hearts in words which if captured in writing might not contain the most accurate vocabulary nor the best syntax. At times we may benefit from a set prayer; at other times we may be blessed by extemporaneous expression.

Not confined to a schedule. Unlike "foxhole Christians" who pray only in danger, Jesus prayed both at regular hours and in critical situations. When difficulty crossed His path, He went immediately to prayer. He prayed both in calm and in crisis. His praying was determined as much by emergency as by chronology. Significant events sent Him to prayer; e.g., His baptism, His choice of apostles, the Gethsemane ordeal, and the cross. He prayed at the start of matters, as He did before beginning His earthly ministry, early in the morning, and before performing His miracles.

Every danger should drive us to pray. We should program our prayer computer so that the moment trouble looms on the horizon we immediately lift our hearts to God for help. Prayer should be our first reaction, not our last resort.

Not rigid in duration. Jesus rebuked vain repetitions. To say the same words over and over meaninglessly was just mouthing prayers. He would not look with favor on the person who mechanically repeated "Lord Jesus Christ, Son of God, have mercy on me, a sinner" constantly day after day. He warned that we would not be heard because of our much speaking. He also castigated the Pharisees for making long prayers in a pretense of piety, while at the same time engaged in cheating poor widows.

But Jesus did not forbid lengthy praying per se. On at least two occasions He prayed long—an all-night prayer session, and the hour in Gethsemane. He had compelling reasons for prolonged prayer both times. The all-night vigil preceded His far-reaching choice of apostles on whom depended, from a human standpoint, the success of His mission.

His hour of prayer in Gethsemane may well have been His usual practice. He spoke of watching with Him one hour. On the night before the cross, under such emotional intensity, who could fault Him for praying as long as He could. But many of His prayers were spontaneous outbursts, often just a sentence or two. Even His High Priestly Prayer takes no longer than four minutes to read aloud in the English version. Jesus may have prayed at length on many occasions, just as many times He prayed briefly.

For us to pray like Jesus doesn't mean a specific duration for each prayer. A half-hour isn't necessarily more spiritual than ten minutes. Five minutes may be more effectual than an hour. We should pray as long as we need to spend time in the Father's presence. Different people will tend toward different habits. Many find it profitable to have several short spans of prayer each day, rather than one long session.

Not restricted to any posture. Since Jesus prayed spontaneously in emergency situations, He prayed in varying positions: emerging from the baptismal waters of the Jordan, looking upwards, standing, seated, kneeling, prostrate on the ground, on the cross, with lifted hands.

For some, religious position is mandatory. One man, whose belief required him to point in a specific direction, carried a compass to help him maintain his bearings on a train, twisting and curving in its climb up a mountain side.

For Jesus, externals were unimportant—it was the heart attitude that mattered. Not beauty of language, nor location, nor hour of day, nor length of time, nor number of repetitions, nor position of body, but the spirit within. A man who fell down a well and ended up with his feet pointing to the sky, said, "The prayingest prayer I ever prayed was a-standing on my head."

Jesus Accomplished the Father's Will Through Prayer

Jesus' praying was not just a devotional exercise at a regular time in a quiet place, nor a cry for help in crisis times. Rather, it was His way of getting things done.

Jesus petitioned His Father. Though several Greek verbs are translated "pray" in the Gospels, the word most often used of Jesus' praying means to make a request of God, to implore His aid in some particular matter. This petitionary verb is used of His praying at His baptism, early in the morning, in the hills, before choosing the apostles, after feeding the five thousand, at the transfiguration, when His disciples asked to be taught to pray, to bless little children, and in Gethsemane.

A verb meaning "bless" is used also of little children, and before the feeding of both the five thousand and the four thousand, at the Last Supper, at the meal in Emmaus, and at the Ascension.

A verb meaning "thank" is used also at the feeding of the four thousand, at the last Supper, and before Lazarus' raising.

The Gospel of John omits many incidents of Jesus at prayer, perhaps because prayer is so human a practice, and John is stressing His deity. When John does speak of Jesus at prayer, he uses verbs like "say" or "ask," which more or less imply equality between the one praying and the one prayed to. But the verb used most of all has the idea of petitioning.

Jesus petitioned His Father for spiritual matters. Prayer was Jesus' way of accomplishing things. What things? Everything that promoted the kingdom and will of God. The Father's program called for the defeat of Satan's kingdom through the power of the cross and the resurrection, and for the ultimate ushering in of the Father's reign when the kingdoms of this world become the kingdoms of our God and of His Christ.

Jesus came to earth to do His Father's bidding. Leaving heaven to come as a baby, He said, "I have come to do your will, O God" (Heb. 10:7). All four Gospels begin with the same announcement—the divine kingdom is at hand. To help fulfill His mission Jesus saturated His life with prayer. He knew full well the reality and power of Satan. The thrust of His praying is found in His model prayer, "your kingdom come, your will be done on earth as it is in heaven" (Matt. 6:10). The night before He died, He prayed, "Not my will, but yours be done." He also declared at the end, "I have brought you glory on earth by completing the work you gave me to do" (John 17:4).

Praying was Jesus' way of advancing the kingdom. Luke mentions Jesus' frequent withdrawals to lonely places to pray (5:16), then in the next verse, speaking of subsequent ministry to the multitudes converging on Him, says, "And the power of the Lord was present for him to heal the sick" (v. 17). Then Luke immediately relates the healing of the paralytic let down through the roof of a house (v. 18ff).

Matthew records that after Jesus fed and dismissed the five thousand, "he went up on a mountainside by himself to pray" (14:23). The next verse begins the story of His walking on water to calm the storm for His struggling disciples. The *International Standard Bible Encyclopedia* comments, "Here perhaps lies an explanation of the true significance of the miraculous. The communion of the Lord with a supreme Father had filled the physical nature of Jesus with spiritual forces which extended the power of the spirit over the material world beyond the limits by which man is bound in his normal and sinful condition."[4]

Prayer was more than an attitude for Him, it was also an act of petitioning for something specific—asking, seeking, knocking, often urgently, perseveringly, and emotionally.

Jesus asked for specific things and gave reasons for His requests. Frequently our prayers are a general "God bless" so-and-so. No specific blessing is requested, and no reason is given for the request. But vagueness did not characterize Jesus' praying. In many of His directly quoted prayers He gives not only a request, but the explanation for the request as well.

For example, at Lazarus' grave He prayed for the raising of Lazarus so that those hearing the petition might believe that Jesus was sent by the Father.

He prayed for Peter to maintain his faith so that the apostle would become a tower of strength to the church.

Jesus asked for the unity of His followers so that the world might know that the Father had sent Him.

On the cross Jesus prayed, "Father, forgive them, for they do not know what they are doing." Curtis C. Mitchell comments, "Notice that amid the pain and turmoil, Christ was still careful to explain to the Father the reason for making the request! This feature has been typical of all of Christ's prayers, and its presence at this point seems to indicate a fixed habit. A man having nails driven through his hands would hardly be expected to pray for others in the first place, much less to state a reason for making the request! Jesus was not in the habit of rattling off a string of bare petitions the way we would read a grocery list. He always stated reasons and evidently this fixed habit prevailed even in this unlikely context."[5]

Jesus helped answer His own prayers. He put feet to His prayers. Not only did He pray for Lazarus' raising, but with a loud voice called Him forth from the dead. He not only prayed that Peter's faith not fail, but He warned him beforehand, then after the denial sought Peter out privately to restore him, and later elicited from Peter a threefold affirmation of love in the presence of other disciples at a meal on the Galilean shores.

Sometimes we can do nothing to help answer our prayers, but often we can. Billy Sunday said, "If you're praying for a job, God expects you to read the want ads." The farmer who prays for a harvest must sow the seed and cultivate it. C. S. Lewis wrote, "I am often, I believe, praying for others when I should be doing things for them. It's so much easier to pray for a bore than to go and see him."[6]

Jesus asked for matters agreeable to His Father's will. Jesus' consuming passion was to do the will of the one who sent Him (John 4:34; 5:30). His requests were unswervingly directed toward those items that would help Him fulfill His task.

As His followers, we should be asking for matters agreeable to His will. Jesus told us how we could do this: "If you remain in me and my words remain in you, ask whatever you wish, and it will be given you" (John 15:7). Note, "If . . . my words remain in you." The key is our saturation with Christ's words. If His words abide in us, then His thoughts become our thoughts, His ways our ways, His desires our desires, and His will our will. Abiding is really our saying, "Thy will be done." Petitions offered by an abiding believer are granted.

Praying in the will of God has been likened to a sailor nearing shore and throwing out a rope to someone on shore who will tie the rope around a post. The sailor does not pull the shore to the boat, but pulls himself and all on board to the shore. It has been said, "Prayer is not pulling God to my will, but the aligning of my will to the will of God." Someone once prayed, "Lord, put on my heart what You have on Yours."

Praying in Jesus' name is another way of praying in God's will. Praying in Jesus' name is not a fixed phrase to end our prayer, nor a magic wand to wave over a prayer to gain an automatic answer. Praying in Jesus' name means praying not only in the merits of Jesus Christ, but also in His interests, for Jesus' sake, for things He wants, for His program, for His honor, for His benefit, for the furtherance of His kingdom, for His glory. Such praying comes from abiding, obedient hearts. To tack the name of Jesus to the end our requests for things that reflect our own selfish desires and not the furtherance of Jesus' work is to misuse Jesus' name. A Scottish catechism says, "Prayer is an offering up of our desires to God for things agreeable to His will, in the name of Christ with confession of our sins and thankful acknowledgment of His mercies."

Directly or indirectly Jesus' petitions always concerned the advance of His kingdom, the glory of God, the accomplishing of the Father's will. His prayers were always answered. He used prayer to accomplish the Father's will. Three times the Father's voice thundered approval of His beloved Son; each time the Son had been praying. Prayer was the instrument that opened heaven.

Likewise we are to ask for matters that promote God's work. C. H. Spurgeon said, "Whether we like it or not, asking is the rule of the kingdom." The omnipotent God of the universe deigns to answer prayer because we ask. He revels in our requesting. A Korean pastor kept a record of his prayer requests, noting the answers. He titled the volume, *The Book of the Kingdom of God.*

Jesus seemed to pray more for the sanctification of saints than for the salvation of sinners. His prayer on the cross, "Father, forgive them," was one of the few occasions when He prayed for the lost. His usual policy was to pray for believers, as in His High Priestly Prayer, "I am not praying for the world, but for those you have given me, . . ." (John 17:9). He prayed for believers to display unity among themselves so that the world mighty believe that the Father had sent Him (v. 21). Observable love among the saints would exhibit the trademark of genuine Christianity and create an evangelistic atmosphere.

During the Italian occupation of Ethiopia in the days of Mussolini, believers suffered considerable persecution. But in his book, *Fire on the Mountain*, Raymond Davis reports that the love demonstrated by believers for each other during their suffering made a major impression on unbelievers. For example, no government provision was made for feeding prisoners in jail. This was left to relatives and friends. Believers in the prisons were so well cared for by fellow believers that enough food remained to to feed the non-Christian prisoners too, who otherwise would have starved. Such kindness was previously unknown. As a result of this demonstrated love word spread far and wide. Unbelievers sought out believers to learn more about the Christian faith. Many became Christians, and on their release went back home and attended the nearest church.[7]

Naturally we should pray for our unsaved family and friends. But we should also keep in mind that Jesus placed emphasis on the development of Christian character which prepared believers to announce the gospel to the lost around them. Jesus urged his followers to pray to the Lord of the harvest to send forth laborers into the fields. In remembering our unsaved loved ones we need to pray that some faithful brother or sister will cross their path with a loving witness.

Sadly today Christians often fail to develop relationships with non-Christians. Evangelist Larry Moyer points out that one reason is today's automation. "A person can now turn into his driveway, open his garage door with his automatic door opener, drive in, and close the garage door without ever saying hello to his next-door neighbor who is painting the front door. Banking by telephone encourages seclusion even more. By 'reaching out and touching someone,' you can pay your bills, apply for credit, invest in the stock market, and transfer funds without talking to anyone face-to-face. . . . Even a pizza can be delivered to your home by an employee who can't be there longer than thirty seconds."[8] He also noted that most suburban backyards are enclosed by fences high enough to prevent striking up conversations, and that nearly half of all Americans do not know who their next-door neighbor is.

As we pray for the lost, we should also pray for workers who will make contact with them, at the same time readying our own hearts to share the gospel with those whom the Lord may send across our path.

Jesus supported His prayers with an obedient life. Jesus' prayers were effective because they were backed by obedient conduct. Jesus warned that prayers are hindered by lack of faith, ostentation, mindlessness, and hypocrisy. But none of these imperfections marred His praying.

Praying cannot be divorced from living. Zeal cannot end with words but must extend to deeds. We cannot follow Jesus in prayer unless we follow Him in compliance. Andrew Murray in *With Christ in the School of Prayer* wrote, "The effective prayer of faith comes from a life given up to the will and the love of God. Not as a result of what I try to be when praying, but because of what I am when I'm not praying, is my prayer answered by God."[9]

Prayer in National Situations

At times in our national annals, lawlessness, violence, and immorality have been rampant, and church life at low ebb. But history records times when prayer meetings sprang up and spread from coast to coast, bringing revitalization to the church and renewed morality to the nation.

During the two days after the April 1992 Los Angeles riots, New York City braced for a similar tumult. Rumors ran wild, nearly clearing out Manhattan on Friday afternoon. TV news crews poised for action. Instead networks reported a more amazing story—no riots in New York. *Metro Prayer Report*, which promotes metropolitan concerts of prayer, told how one news crew, desperate for a story, interviewed people in Harlem, Bronx, and Brooklyn, and everywhere got the same answer, "We're praying."

A month before the riots, pastors of four large evangelical churches canceled their regular Sunday evening service, asking their people to come to church and pray for New York. Feeling more urgency, they opened their churches nightly. Often one-thousand persons would spend the evening praying for the city's needs. *Metro Prayer Report* also related that at the same time thirty churches linked together for a 30-day "Lord's Watch," during which intercessors from a different church would "stand watch" in prayer on behalf of the city. The day after the L.A. riots broke out, a weekend of eight Community Concerts of Prayer involved three hundred metro churches. Leaders concluded that these prayer meetings had a special depth as people prayed for the poor, for racial harmony, and for God's protection for the city.

Too often we wish the Lord to do unusual things for us while failing to spend serious energy in prayer. To pray today Jesus' way requires discipline, obedience, fervency, spontaneity, specificity, and perseverance.

Notes

1. Howard Taylor, *Hudson Taylor's Spiritual Secret* (Chicago: Moody Press, 1965), p. 235.
2. *My Life: A Guided Tour*, p. 349.
3. *The Life of Prayer*, p. 110.
4. L. D. Bevan, "Prayers of Jesus," *ISBE* (Grand Rapids: Wm. B. Eerdmans), p. 2431.
5. *Praying Jesus' Way*, p. 69.
6. *Letters to Malcolm.*
7. Raymond Davis, *Fire on the Mountain* (Grand Rapids: Zondervan, 1966).

8. Larry Moyer, *Toolbox*, Spring 1993.
9. Andrew Murray, *With Christ in the School of Prayer* (Springdale, Pa.: Whitaker House, 1981).

Bibliography

Barker, William P. *To Pray Is To Live.* Old Tappan, N.J.:Revell, 1977.

Barnes, Albert. *Notes on the Old and New Testament.* Grand Rapids: Baker, 1974.

Baxter, Richard. *The Saints' Everlasting Rest.* London: Epworth, 1962.

Beers, V. Gilbert. Tape of Luncheon Address at NAE Annual Convention in Columbus, Ohio, March, 1985.

Bounds, E. M. *Power Through Prayer.* Grand Rapids: Zondervan, 1979.

Calvin, John. *Sermons on Ephesus.* Edinburgh: Banner of Truth Trust, 1975.

Carrell, Dr. Alexis. *Robins Reader.* Richmond, Va.: A. H. Robins Co., Inc. January 1954.

Davis, Raymond. *Fire On The Mountains.* Grand Rapids: Zondervan, 1966.

Dick, Lois Hoadley. *Isobel Kuhn.* Minneapolis: Bethany House, 1987.

Duewel, Wesley. *Touch the World Through Prayer.* Grand Rapids: Francis Asbury Press of Zondervan, 1986.

Eastman, Dick. *The Hour That Changes the World.* Grand Rapids: Baker, 1978.

Edersheim, *The Life and Times of Jesus The Messiah.* Grand Rapids: Wm. B. Eerdmans, 1943.

Erdman, Charles. *The Gospel of Luke.* Louisville: Westminster Press, 1943.

Foster, Richard J. *Prayer: Finding the Heart's True Home.* San Francisco: HarperCollins, 1992.

Godet, F. L. *Commentary on the Gospel of Luke* Vol. 1. Grand Rapids: Zondervan, n.d.

Hampton, Vinita and Carol Pleuddemann. *World Shapers: A Treasury of Quotes from Great Missionaries.* Wheaton: Harold Shaw Publishers, 1991.

Hensley, Dennis E. "The 'Jesus Pattern' of Prayer." *The War Cry* (December 8, 1990).

International Standard Bible Encyclopedia. Grand Rapids: Wm. B. Eerdmans, 1939.

Johnson, Edmund L. "This Thing Called Prayer." *Guideposts* (May 1991).

Lemcio, Miriam Payne. *Deo Volente.* Houghton College, 1987.

Lewis, H. Lewis. *Biblical Reflections,* Winter 1994.

Lewis, C. S. *Letters to Malcolm: Chiefly on Prayer.* New York: Harcourt, Brace & World, 1964.

Lindsell, Harold. *Missionary Principles and Practice.* Old Tappan, N.J.: Revell, 1955.

Lockyer, Herbert. *Last Words of Saints and Sinners.* Grand Rapids: Kregel, 1969.

Martin, William. *A Prophet with Honor.* New York: William Morrow & Co., 1991.

Mason, David E. *Frank C. Laubach, Teacher of Millions.* Minneapolis: T. S. Denison Co., 1967.

Mitchell, Curtis C. *Praying Jesus' Way.* Old Tappan, N.J.: Revell, 1991.

Montgomery, Helen Barrrett. *Centenary Translation of the New Testament.* American Baptist Publication Society, 1924.

Morgan, G. Campbell. *The Gospel According to Luke.* Old Tappan, N.J.: Revell 1931.

Murray, Andrew. *With Christ in the School of Prayer.* Springdale, Pa.: Whitaker House, 1981.

Papini, Giovanni. *The Life of Christ.* New York: Harcourt, Brace & Co., 1923.

Prayers: New and Old. Cincinnati: Forward Movement Publications, n.d.

Pulpit Commentary, Funk and Wagnalls, n.d.

Robertson, A. T. *A Translation of Luke's Gospel.* New York: Doran, 1923.

Robinson, Haddon. *Jesus' Blueprint For Prayer.* Grand Rapids: Radio Bible Class, 1989.

Sayer, George. *Jack: C. S. Lewis and His Times.* New York: Harper & Row, 1988.

Schaeffer, Edith. *The Life of Prayer.* Wheaton: Crossway Books, 1992.

Simpson, A. B. *When The Comforter Came.* Camp Hill, Pa.: Christian Publications, 1911.

Strong, John Henry. *Jesus, The Man of Prayer.* Valley Forge, Pa.: Judson, 1945.

Taylor, Howard. *Hudson Taylor's Spiritual Secret.* Chicagp: Moody, 1965.

Taylor, Kenneth N. with Virginia Muir. *My Life: A Guided Tour.* Wheaton: Tyndale, 1991.

Whiston, Charles. *Pray: A Study in Distinctive Christian Praying*. Grand Rapids: Wm. B. Eerdmans, 1972.

White, John. *The Fight*. Downers Grove, Ill.: InterVarsity, 1976.

Williams, Pat and Jill with Jerry Jenkins. *Rekindled*. Old Tappan, N.J.: Revell, 1985.